Groundwater Quality in Western New York, 2011

By James E. Reddy

Prepared in cooperation with the
New York State Department of Environmental Conservation

Open-File Report 2013–1095

U.S. Department of the Interior
U.S. Geological Survey

U.S. Department of the Interior
SALLY JEWELL, Secretary

U.S. Geological Survey
Suzette M. Kimball, Acting Director

U.S. Geological Survey, Reston, Virginia: 2013

For more information on the USGS—the Federal source for science about the Earth, its natural and living resources, natural hazards, and the environment, visit http://www.usgs.gov or call 1–888–ASK–USGS.

For an overview of USGS information products, including maps, imagery, and publications, visit http://www.usgs.gov/pubprod

To order this and other USGS information products, visit http://store.usgs.gov

Suggested citation:
Reddy, J.E., 2013, Groundwater quality in western New York, 2011: U.S. Geological Survey Open-File Report 2013–1095, 28 p., at http://pubs.usgs.gov/of/2013/1095/.

Contents

Figure

Tables

Conversion Factors, Datum, and Abbreviations

Multiply	By	To obtain
Length		
inch (in.)	2.54	centimeter (cm)
foot (ft)	0.3048	meter (m)
Area		
square mile (mi²)	2.590	square kilometer (km²)
Volume		
million gallons (Mgal)	3,785	cubic meter (m³)
Flow rate		
gallon per minute (gal/min)	0.06309	liter per second (L/s)
gallon per day (gal/d)	0.003785	cubic meter per day (m³/d)
million gallons per day (Mgal/d)	0.04381	cubic meter per second (m³/s)
inch per year (in/yr)	25.4	millimeter per year (mm/yr)
Radioactivity		
picocurie per liter (pCi/L)	0.037	becquerel per liter (Bq/L)

Temperature in degrees Celsius (°C) may be converted to degrees Fahrenheit (°F) as follows:

°F=(1.8×°C)+32

Temperature in degrees Fahrenheit (°F) may be converted to degrees Celsius (°C) as follows:

°C=(°F-32)/1.8

Vertical coordinate information is referenced to the National Geodetic Vertical Datum of 1929 (NGVD 29).

Horizontal coordinate information is referenced to the North American Datum of 1983 (NAD 83).

Specific conductance is given in microsiemens per centimeter at 25 degrees Celsius (μS/cm at 25°C).

Concentrations of chemical constituents in water are given either in milligrams per liter (mg/L) or micrograms per liter (μg/L).

Abbreviations

AMCL	alternative maximum contaminant level
CFCL	USGS Chlorofluorocarbon Laboratory
CFU/mL	colony-forming units per milliliter
LRL	laboratory reporting level
MCL	maximum contaminant level
NWQL	USGS National Water Quality Laboratory
NYSDEC	New York State Department of Environmental Conservation
NYSDOH	New York State Department of Health
Pt-Co units	platinum-cobalt units

QC	quality control
SDWS	secondary drinking-water standard
THM	trihalomethane
USEPA	U.S. Environmental Protection Agency
USGS	U.S. Geological Survey
VOC	volatile organic compound

Groundwater Quality in Western New York, 2011

By James E. Reddy

Abstract

Water samples collected from 16 production wells and 15 private residential wells in western New York from July through November 2011 were analyzed to characterize the groundwater quality. Fifteen of the wells were finished in sand and gravel aquifers, and 16 were finished in bedrock aquifers. Six of the 31 wells were sampled in a previous western New York study, which was conducted in 2006. Water samples from the 2011 study were analyzed for 147 physiochemical properties and constituents that included major ions, nutrients, trace elements, radionuclides, pesticides, volatile organic compounds (VOCs), and indicator bacteria. Results of the water-quality analyses are presented in tabular form for individual wells, and summary statistics for specific constituents are presented by aquifer type. The results are compared with Federal and New York State drinking-water standards, which typically are identical. The results indicate that groundwater generally is of acceptable quality, although at 30 of the 31 wells sampled, at least one of the following constituents was detected at a concentration that exceeded current or proposed Federal or New York State drinking-water standards: pH (two samples), sodium (eight samples), sulfate (three samples), total dissolved solids (nine samples), aluminum (two samples), arsenic (one sample), iron (ten samples), manganese (twelve samples), radon-222 (sixteen samples), benzene (one sample), and total coliform bacteria (nine samples). Existing drinking-water standards for color, chloride, fluoride, nitrate, nitrite, antimony, barium, beryllium, cadmium, chromium, copper, lead, mercury, selenium, silver, thallium, zinc, gross alpha radioactivity, uranium, fecal coliform, *Escherichia coli*, and heterotrophic bacteria were not exceeded in any of the samples collected. None of the pesticides analyzed exceeded existing drinking-water standards.

Introduction

Section 305(b) of the Federal Clean Water Act Amendments of 1977 requires that States monitor and report biennially on the chemical quality of surface water and groundwater within State boundaries (U.S. Environmental Protection Agency, 1997). In 2002, the U.S. Geological Survey (USGS) developed a program in cooperation with the New York State Department of Environmental Conservation (NYSDEC) to evaluate groundwater quality throughout the major river basins in New York on a rotating basis. The program parallels the NYSDEC Rotating Intensive Basin Study Program, which evaluates surface-water quality in 2 or 3 of the 14 major river basins in the State each year. The groundwater-quality program began in 2002 with a pilot study in the Mohawk River Basin and has continued throughout upstate New York since then (table 1). Sampling completed in 2008 represented the conclusion of a first round of groundwater-quality sampling throughout New York State (excluding Long Island, which is monitored through county programs). Groundwater-quality sampling was conducted in 2011 in the Mohawk River Basin and the Western Lake Ontario, Lake Erie-Niagara River, and Allegheny River Basins in western New York; these basins also were sampled in 2006 as part of the groundwater program. This report presents the results of the 2011 groundwater study in western New York.

Groundwater characteristics are affected by the geology and the land use of the area. Shallow wells that tap sand and gravel aquifers are susceptible to contamination by several kinds of compounds, including deicing chemicals, nutrients, pesticides, and volatile organic compounds (VOCs) from agricultural, industrial, residential areas, and upgradient highways. The movement of these contaminants to the water table through the soils and surficial sand and gravel can be relatively rapid. Bedrock wells that tap into sandstone and shale aquifers in rural upland areas generally are less susceptible to contamination from industrial and urban sources, which are mainly in the valleys; but bedrock wells in lowland areas underlain by carbonate bedrock (limestone and dolostone; Eckhardt and others, 2008), may be more vulnerable to contamination from surface runoff because infiltration rates and groundwater flow can be relatively rapid through bedrock solution features. Agricultural land upgradient of wells may be a potential source of contamination by fecal waste from livestock, fertilizers, and pesticides; lawns and residential septic systems also are a potential source of these contaminants. In addition to anthropogenic contaminants, the aquifers contain naturally derived constituents that may diminish water quality, such as arsenic, chloride, hydrogen sulfide, iron, manganese, methane, radon gas, sodium, and sulfate.

Table 1. Previous groundwater-quality studies and reports for New York State.

Study area	Year	Report	Reference
Mohawk River Basin	2002	Water-Data Report NY–02–1	Butch and others, 2003
Chemung River Basin	2003	Open-File Report 2004–1329	Hetcher-Aguila, 2005
Lake Champlain Basin	2004	Open-File Report 2006–1088	Nystrom, 2006
Upper Susquehanna River Basin	2004–5	Open-File Report 2006–1161	Hetcher-Aguila and Eckhardt, 2006
Delaware River Basin	2005–6	Open-File Report 2007–1098	Nystrom, 2007b
Genesee River Basin	2005–6	Open-File Report 2007–1093	Eckhardt and others, 2007
St. Lawrence River Basin	2005–6	Open-File Report 2007–1066	Nystrom, 2007a
Mohawk River Basin	2006	Open-File Report 2008–1086	Nystrom, 2008
Western New York	2006	Open-File Report 2008–1140	Eckhardt and others, 2008
Central New York	2007	Open-File Report 2009–1257	Eckhardt and others, 2009
Upper Hudson River Basin	2007	Open-File Report 2009–1240	Nystrom, 2009
Eastern Lake Ontario Basin	2008	Open-File Report 2011–1074	Risen and Reddy, 2011a
Chemung River Basin	2008	Open-File Report 2011–1112	Risen and Reddy, 2011b
Lower Hudson River Basin	2008	Open-File Report 2010–1197	Nystrom, 2010
Lake Champlain Basin	2009	Open-File Report 2011–1180	Nystrom, 2011
Upper Susquehanna River Basin	2009	Open-File Report 2012–1045	Reddy and Risen, 2012
Delaware River Basin	2010	Open-File Report 2011–1320	Nystrom, 2012
St. Lawrence River Basin	2010	Open-File Report 2011–1320	Nystrom, 2012
Genesee River Basin	2010	Open-File Report 2012–1135	Reddy, 2012
Mohawk River Basin	2011	Open-File Report 2013–1021	Nystrom and Scott, 2013

Purpose and Scope

This report supplements the water-quality study completed in 2006 for western New York (Eckhardt and others, 2008) by resampling 6 of the production wells from that study (AG 265, E1903, E1904, GS 216, OL 19, and WO 351) and provides analytical results for 25 new wells (fig. 1). This report briefly describes the study area and the sampling methods and presents results of the water-quality analyses for the 31 wells sampled in 2011. Summary statistics of the number of samples exceeding Federal or State drinking-water standards and the minimum, median, and maximum concentrations of selected analytes in sand and gravel and bedrock aquifers are provided in tables 2 through 4; information on the sampled wells and detailed analytical results for all analytes are provided in the appendix (tables 1–1 through 1–9).

Study Area

The 5,340-square mile (mi^2) study area includes all or parts of the nine westernmost counties of New York (fig. 1). It encompasses parts of the Lake Erie and Niagara River Basin, the western Lake Ontario Basin (between the Niagara River and Genesee River Basins), and the Allegheny River Basin (fig. 1). The parts of these drainage basins that lie outside

New York's boundaries were not included in this study. A complete description of the study area is included in Eckhardt and others (2008).

The central, southern, and eastern parts of the study area lie within the Appalachian Plateau physiographic province (fig. 1), the northern part lies in the Lake Ontario Lowlands province, and the western part lies in the Lake Erie Lowlands province. Forest and pasture dominate the uplands and narrow valleys of the southern and eastern parts of the study area; cultivation of row crops, apples, and grapes is common in the Lake Erie and Lake Ontario lowlands; and row-crop, forage-crop, and dairy farming are concentrated in a band of fertile soils between Buffalo and Rochester. The Buffalo and Niagara Falls metropolitan area lies near the outlet of Lake Erie and extends northward along the Niagara River. The study area contains several small lakes, such as Chautauqua Lake, and is crossed by the New York State Barge (Erie) Canal, which traverses the State from Albany to Buffalo.

During deglaciation of the region, sand and gravel were deposited by meltwater streams, and clay, silt, and fine sand were deposited in proglacial lakes. The glaciofluvial and glaciolacustrine deposits within the study area are described in detail by Coates (1966) and Randall (2001). The most productive aquifers within the study area are the glaciofluvial deposits of sand and gravel in the valleys. Bedrock aquifers

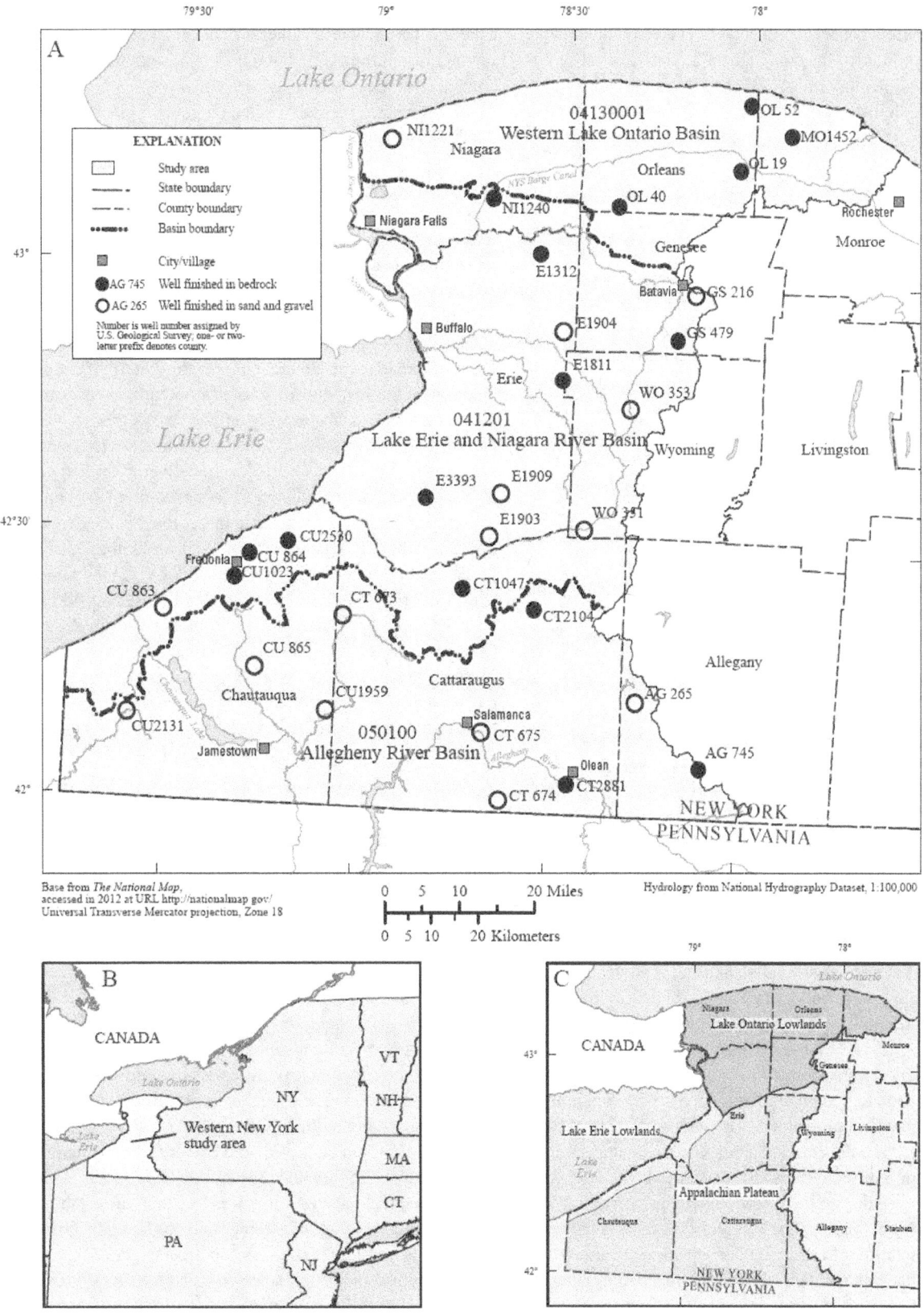

Figure 1. *A*, pertinent geographic features of study area in western New York and locations of the 31 wells sampled in 2011 and *B*, general location and *C*, physiographic features of the study area. Well data are listed in table 1–1.

typically are used for water supply in upland areas where sand and gravel aquifers generally are absent. The bedrock aquifers throughout most of the study area are relatively flat-lying interbedded sedimentary units of shale, siltstone, sandstone, limestone, and dolostone of Silurian and Devonian age (Fisher and others, 1970).

Methods

A total of 31 wells (table 1–1) were selected for sample collection as described by Eckhardt and others (2008)—15 were finished in sand and gravel aquifers and 16 were finished in bedrock aquifers. Of the 15 wells that tap into sand and gravel aquifers, 13 are production wells and 2 are private residential wells. Of the 16 bedrock wells, 3 are production wells and 13 are private residential wells. Samples were collected from July through November 2011. The water samples were analyzed for 147 physiochemical properties and constituents that included major ions, nutrients, trace elements, radionuclides, pesticides, VOCs, and indicator bacteria.

Wells were selected to provide adequate spatial coverage of the study area. The study did not target specific municipalities, industries, or agricultural practices. The private residential wells were selected on the basis of information from the NYSDEC Water Well Program, which began in 2000. Production wells were selected using information from the NYSDEC Water Well Program and the New York State Department of Health (NYSDOH) Drinking Water Protection Program.

Most of the wells that are finished in sand and gravel were in the valleys and ranged from 36 to 177 feet (ft) deep (table 1–1). The wells that are finished in bedrock were generally in the uplands and ranged from 25 to 218 ft deep; all the bedrock wells were finished in sedimentary units of shale, siltstone, sandstone, limestone, dolostone, and evaporites (table 1–1).

In addition to the 31 groundwater samples, three quality control (QC) samples—two field blanks and one concurrent replicate sample—were collected. The QC blank samples contained no constituents in concentrations greater than the laboratory reporting levels (LRLs) except silica, boron, and iron (unfiltered), which were detected at trace concentrations. This indicates that little to no contamination occurred through the sampling or analytical procedures. The variability between the replicate sample and the corresponding environmental sample was greatest for unfiltered trace elements. The LRL is generally equal to twice the annual determined long-term method detection level (LT–MDL). The LRL controls false negative error. The probability of falsely reporting a nondetection result for a sample that contained an analyte at a concentration equal to or greater than the LRL is predicted to be less than or equal to 1 percent. The value of the LRL is indicated as less than (<) for samples in which the analyte was not detected. The USGS National Water Quality Laboratory (NWQL) in Denver, Colorado, collects quality-control data from selected analytical

methods on a continuing basis to determine LT–MDLs and to establish LRLs. These values are reevaluated annually based on the most current quality-control data, and, therefore, may change (Childress and others, 1999).

Three pesticides were detected in the replicate sample; deethylatrazine (CIAT) and prometon at estimated concentrations of 0.001 micrograms per liter (μg/L), and atrazine at an estimated concentration of 0.003 μg/L. The concentrations of these three pesticides were identical in the corresponding environmental sample except for atrazine, which was detected at an estimated concentration of 0.002 μg/L in the environmental sample.

Groundwater-sample collection and processing followed standard USGS procedures as documented in the National Field Manual for the Collection of Water-Quality Data (U.S. Geological Survey, variously dated). All samples except those for radionuclide analyses were chilled to 4 degrees Celsius (°C) or less and were kept chilled until delivery to the analyzing laboratory. The samples were delivered directly or shipped by overnight delivery to four laboratories: (1) the NWQL for analysis of inorganic major ions, nutrients, total organic carbon, inorganic trace elements, radon-222, pesticides and pesticide degradates, and VOCs; (2) the USGS Chlorofluorocarbon Laboratory (CFCL) in Reston, Virginia, for select dissolved gases; (3) Eberline Services in Richmond, California, for gross-alpha and gross-beta radioactivities; and (4) a NYSDOH-certified laboratory in Depew, New York, for bacterial analysis. Physiochemical properties, such as water temperature, pH, dissolved oxygen concentration, and specific conductance, were measured at the sampling site.

Groundwater Quality

Samples from 31 wells were analyzed for 147 physiochemical properties and constituents. Many of these (65) were not detected above the LRLs in any sample (table 1–2). Results for the remaining 82 physiochemical properties and constituents that were detected are presented in tables 1–3 through 1–9. The categories of physiochemical properties and the concentrations of constituents are presented in appendix 1 as follows: physiochemical properties in table 1–3, major ions in table 1–4, nutrients and total organic carbon in table 1–5, trace elements and radionuclides in table 1–6, pesticides in table 1–7, VOCs in table 1–8, and bacterial water-quality indicators in table 1–9. Some concentrations were reported as estimated when the detected value was less than the established LRL or when recovery of a compound has been documented to be highly variable (Childress and others, 1999).

Analytical results for selected constituents were compared with Federal and New York State drinking-water standards, which are typically identical. The standards include maximum contaminant levels (MCLs) and secondary drinking-water standards (SDWS) established by the U.S. Environmental Protection Agency (USEPA; U.S. Environmental

Protection Agency, 1999, 2002, 2009) and the NYSDOH (New York State Department of Health, 2011). The MCLs are enforceable standards that specify the highest level of a contaminant that is allowed in public-water drinking supplies; they are not enforceable for private residential wells but are presented here as a guideline for evaluation of the water-quality results. The SDWS are nonenforceable guidelines and are based on cosmetic and aesthetic criteria, such as taste, odor, or staining of plumbing fixtures.

The quality of the sampled groundwater generally was acceptable, although in samples from 30 of the 31 wells, the concentration of at least one constituent exceeded recommended MCLs or SDWSs set by the USEPA or the NYSDOH. Exceedances generally involved minerals and chemical elements that occur from natural interactions of water and rock (aluminum, arsenic, iron, manganese, radon-222, sodium, and sulfate) but also included benzene, which is a VOC, and total coliform bacteria contamination.

Physiochemical Properties

The color values for all samples (table 1–3) were less than 1 platinum-cobalt (Pt-Co) unit (the LRL) except for one sample from a bedrock well with a value of 2 Pt-Co units. The NYSDOH MCL and USEPA SDWS of 15 Pt-Co units were not exceeded in any sample. The pH of the samples ranged from 6.0 to 8.7; the median was 7.6 for sand and gravel wells and 7.4 for bedrock wells. Two of the 31 wells had pH values outside the accepted USEPA SDWS range of 6.5 to 8.5: a pH of 6.0 was detected at a sand and gravel well, and a pH of 8.7 was detected at a bedrock well (U.S. Environmental Protection Agency, 2009). The specific conductance of the samples ranged from 138 to 2,450 microsiemens per centimeter (μS/cm) at 25 °C; the median was 454 μS/cm at 25 °C for sand and gravel wells and 592 μS/cm at 25 °C for bedrock wells. The temperature of the water ranged from 8.7 to 19.3 °C; the median was 12.1 °C for sand and gravel wells and 12.8 °C for bedrock wells.

Dissolved-oxygen concentrations ranged from 0.2 to 8.1 milligrams per liter (mg/L); the median was 3.1 mg/L for sand and gravel wells and 0.5 mg/L for bedrock wells. Methane concentrations ranged from less than 0.0005 (the LRL) to 29.5 mg/L; the median was 0.003 mg/L for sand and gravel wells and 0.024 mg/L for bedrock wells. The odor of hydrogen sulfide gas, which may occur in the absence of oxygen, was noted by field personnel in water from five sand and gravel wells and seven bedrock wells.

Major Ions

The cations that were detected in the greatest concentrations were calcium and sodium (tables 2, 1–4). Calcium concentrations ranged from 2.26 to 485 mg/L; the median was 54.2 mg/L for sand and gravel wells and 71.7 mg/L for bedrock wells. Magnesium concentrations ranged from 0.51 to 65.6 mg/L; the median was 11.0 mg/L for sand and gravel wells and 14.6 mg/L for bedrock wells. Potassium concentrations ranged from 0.64 to 13.5 mg/L; the median was 1.58 mg/L for sand and gravel wells and 1.80 mg/L for bedrock wells. Sodium concentrations ranged from 2.15 to 144 mg/L; the median was 20.3 mg/L for sand and gravel wells and 21.6 mg/L for bedrock wells. The USEPA nonregulatory drinking-water advisory threshold for taste recommends that sodium concentrations in drinking water not exceed the range of 30 to 60 mg/L (U.S. Environmental Protection Agency, 2002, 2009). The concentration of sodium in samples from four sand and gravel wells and five bedrock wells exceeded the upper limit of the USEPA threshold.

The anions that were detected in the greatest concentration were bicarbonate and sulfate (tables 2, 1–4). Bicarbonate concentrations ranged from 45 to 388 mg/L; the median was 207 mg/L for sand and gravel wells and 280 mg/L for bedrock wells. Chloride concentrations ranged from 1.64 to 180 mg/L; the median was 41.1 mg/L for sand and gravel wells and 27.1 mg/L for bedrock wells. Fluoride concentrations ranged from less than 0.04 (the LRL) to 1.17 mg/L; the median was 0.07 mg/L for sand and gravel wells and 0.18 mg/L for bedrock wells. Silica concentrations ranged from 5.92 to 19.4 mg/L; the median was 9.39 mg/L for sand and gravel wells and 12.9 mg/L for bedrock wells. Sulfate concentrations ranged from less than 0.09 mg/L (the LRL) to 1,240 mg/L; the median was 17.2 mg/L for sand and gravel wells and 30.3 mg/L for bedrock wells. The NYSDOH MCL and USEPA SDWS of 250 mg/L for sulfate were exceeded in samples from three bedrock wells.

Calcium and magnesium contribute to water hardness. Water hardness in the basin (tables 2, 1–4) ranged from 7.75 to 1,400 mg/L (as $CaCO_3$); the median was 171 mg/L for sand and gravel wells and 252 mg/L for bedrock wells. Seven of the samples were soft to moderately hard (equal to or less than 120 mg/L as $CaCO_3$) and 24 wells yielded water that was hard to very hard (greater than 120 mg/L as $CaCO_3$) (Hem, 1985). Wells finished in bedrock were slightly more alkaline (median of 229 mg/L as $CaCO_3$) than those finished in sand and gravel (median of 170 mg/L as $CaCO_3$). Concentrations of dissolved solids ranged from 68 to 2,240 mg/L, with a median of 251 mg/L for sand and gravel wells and 340 mg/L for bedrock wells. The USEPA SDWS of 500 mg/L for dissolved solids was exceeded in four sand and gravel wells and five bedrock wells.

Nutrients and Organic Carbon

Nitrate was the predominant nutrient in the groundwater samples (tables 3, 1–5). Concentrations of ammonia ranged from less than 0.010 (the LRL) to 1.01 mg/L as nitrogen (N); the median concentration was 0.011 mg/L as N in samples from sand and gravel wells and 0.078 mg/L as N in samples from bedrock wells. Concentrations of nitrate plus nitrite ranged from less than 0.02 (the LRL) to 2.74 mg/L as N; the

Table 2.   Drinking-water standards and summary statistics for concentrations of major ions in groundwater samples from western New York, 2011.

[All concentrations in milligrams per liter in filtered water. CaCO₃, calcium carbonate; No., number; --, not applicable; <, less than;   C, degrees Celsius]

	Constituent	Drinking-water standard	No. of samples exceeding standard	Sand and gravel (15 samples)			Bedrock (16 samples)		
				Minimum	Median	Maximum	Minimum	Median	Maximum
Cations	Calcium	--	--	19.1	54.2	142	2.26	71.7	485
	Magnesium	--	--	4.58	11.0	30.0	.51	14.6	65.6
	Potassium	--	--	.64	1.58	10.2	.70	1.80	13.5
	Sodium	[1]60	9	2.15	20.3	95.9	3.64	21.6	144
Anions	Bicarbonate	--	--	45	207	360	48	280	388
	Chloride	[2,3]250	0	4.85	41.1	180	1.64	27.1	177
	Fluoride	[4]4.0 [2]2.0 [3]2.2	0	<.04	.07	.46	.04	.18	1.17
	Silica	--	--	5.92	9.39	15.6	6.06	12.9	19.4
	Sulfate	[2,3]250	3	7.07	17.2	127	<.09	30.3	1,240
Hardness as CaCO₃		--	--	69	171	452	7.75	252	1,400
Alkalinity as CaCO₃		--	--	37	170	295	39	229	318
Dissolved solids, dried at 180 °C		[3]500	9	141	251	714	68	340	2,240

[1]U.S. Environmental Protection Agency drinking water advisory taste threshold.

[2]New York State Department of Health maximum contaminant level.

[3]U.S. Environmental Protection Agency secondary drinking water standard.

[4]U.S. Environmental Protection Agency maximum contaminant level.

median concentration was 0.62 mg/L as N in samples from sand and gravel wells and 0.03 mg/L as N in samples from bedrock wells. The concentration of nitrate plus nitrite did not exceed the USEPA and NYSDOH MCLs of 10 mg/L as N in any sample. Nitrite was detected in five samples; the highest concentration was 0.010 mg/L as N. The concentration of nitrite did not exceed the MCL (1 mg/L as N) in any sample. Orthophosphate concentrations ranged from less than 0.004 (the LRL) to 0.035 mg/L as phosphorus (P). Organic carbon was detected in 14 of the 31 samples; the maximum concentration was 1.9 mg/L.

Trace Elements and Radionuclides

The trace elements detected in the greatest concentrations (more than 100 µg/L) were aluminum, barium, boron, copper, iron, lithium, manganese, and strontium (tables 4, 1–6). The largest detected concentration of a trace element, 19,900 µg/L, was of strontium in a sample from a bedrock well. The concentration of aluminum in one sample from a bedrock well, 948 µg/L, exceeded the upper limit of the USEPA SDWS of 200 µg/L. The lower limit of the USEPA SDWS for aluminum (50 µg/L) was exceeded in one sample from a second bedrock well with a concentration of 51 µg/L. The concentration of

arsenic in one sample from a sand and gravel well, 14.1 µg/L, exceeded the USEPA and NYSDOH MCLs of 10 µg/L. The concentration of iron in 9 filtered samples and 10 unfiltered samples exceeded the USEPA SDWS and the NYSDOH MCL of 300 µg/L. The concentration of manganese in 12 filtered samples and 12 unfiltered samples exceeded the USEPA SDWS of 50 µg/L; the NYSDOH MCL of 300 µg/L was exceeded in one filtered sample and one unfiltered sample. Drinking-water standards for antimony, barium, beryllium, cadmium, chromium, copper, lead, mercury, selenium, silver, thallium, uranium, and zinc were not exceeded; additionally, mercury was not detected in any sample (table 1–2).

Three measures of radioactivity were employed (tables 4, 1–6). Gross-alpha activity ranged from less than 0.5 to 3.8 picocuries per liter (pCi/L). The median activity was less than 1.1 pCi/L in samples from sand and gravel wells and 0.9 pCi/L in samples from bedrock wells. The gross-alpha activity did not exceed the USEPA and NYSDOH MCLs of 15 pCi/L in any sample. Gross-beta activity ranged from less than 0.63 to 15.0 pCi/L. The median activity was 1.6 pCi/L in samples from sand and gravel wells and 2.0 pCi/L in samples from bedrock wells. The USEPA and NYSDOH MCLs for gross beta are expressed as a dose of 4 millirems per year; therefore, it cannot be evaluated whether any of the samples

Table 3. Drinking-water standards and summary statistics for concentrations of nutrients in groundwater samples from western New York, 2011.

[All concentrations in milligrams per liter in filtered water except as noted. N, nitrogen; No., number; P, phosphorus; --, not applicable; <, less than]

Constituent	Drinking-water standard	No. of samples exceeding standard	Sand and gravel (15 samples)			Bedrock (16 samples)		
			Minimum	Median	Maximum	Minimum	Median	Maximum
Ammonia plus organic N, as N	--	--	<.05	.08	.28	<.05	.16	1.2
Ammonia, as N	--	--	<.010	.011	.251	<.010	.078	1.01
Nitrate plus nitrite, as N	[1,2]10	0	<.02	.62	1.96	<.02	.03	2.74
Nitrite, as N	[1,2]1	0	<.001	<.001	.001	<.001	<.001	.010
Orthophosphate, as P	--	--	<.004	.009	.035	<.004	.006	.031
Total organic carbon, unfiltered	--	--	<.3	<.5	1.6	<.3	.9	1.9

[1]U.S. Environmental Protection Agency maximum contaminant level.

[2]New York State Department of Health maximum contaminant level.

exceeded the MCL. Radon-222 was detected in every sample, and activity ranged from 56 to 1,880 pCi/L. The median activity was 510 pCi/L in samples from sand and gravel wells and 290 pCi/L in samples from bedrock wells. Radon currently is not regulated in drinking water; however, the USEPA proposed MCL of 300 pCi/L for radon-222 in drinking water was exceeded in 16 samples, but the USEPA proposed alternate maximum contaminant level (AMCL) of 4,000 pCi/L was not exceeded. The AMCL is the proposed allowable activity of radon in raw-water samples where the State has implemented mitigation programs to address the health risks of radon in indoor air. The proposed MCL and AMCL for radon are under review and have not been adopted (Krieger and Whitaker, 1980; U.S. Environmental Protection Agency, 1999, 2009).

Pesticides

Nine pesticides (eight herbicides and one herbicide degradate) were detected in samples from 12 wells (table 1–7). The pesticides were detected in samples from eight sand and gravel wells and four bedrock wells. All pesticide concentrations were in hundredths or thousandths of micrograms per liter. There were a total of 26 pesticide detections; 14 of those have estimated concentrations and 3 detections could not be quantified. The herbicide atrazine was detected in five samples; one of those samples, from a bedrock well, had the highest concentration (0.032 µg/L) of all pesticide detections. The atrazine degradate CIAT is the constituent detected most frequently (10 samples). The sample from one bedrock well (a production well in an agricultural setting) had the most (seven) pesticide detections. None of the pesticides analyzed contained concentrations that exceeded established drinking-water standards.

Volatile Organic Compounds

Thirteen VOCs were detected in samples from four sand and gravel wells and seven bedrock wells (table 1–8). The concentration of benzene in a sample from one private residential bedrock well (56.1 µg/L) exceeded the USEPA and NYSDOH MCLs of 5 µg/L. Benzene was detected in two other bedrock wells at concentrations of 0.1 µg/L and 1.6 µg/L.

Bromodichloromethane, tribromomethane, trichloromethane, and dibromochloromethane were detected in samples from two sand and gravel wells and one bedrock well. These four compounds are trihalomethanes (THMs), which typically are formed as byproducts when chlorine or bromine is used to disinfect water. The maximum THM concentration detected was 4.2 µg/L for dibromochloromethane in a sample from a production sand and gravel well. The concentration of total THMs did not exceed the USEPA and NYSDOH MCLs of 80 µg/L.

Of the remaining VOCs detected, which include 1,1,1-trichloroethane, 1,2-dichloroethane, ethylbenzene, m- + p-Xylene, methyl tert-butyl ether (MTBE), tetrachloroethene, toluene, and trichloroethene, MTBE had the highest concentration at 0.9 µg/L.

Bacteria

All samples were analyzed for total coliform, fecal coliform, Escherichia coli (E. coli), and heterotrophic bacteria. Samples collected on or before September 1, 2011, were analyzed using the presence or absence method; subsequent samples were analyzed using the membrane filtration method. Total coliform bacteria were detected in nine samples (table 1–9): three from sand and gravel wells and six from bedrock wells; six of the positive results were in a presence or absence analysis and the remaining three were in membrane

Table 4. Drinking-water standards and summary statistics for concentrations of trace elements and radionuclides in groundwater samples from western New York, 2011.

[All concentrations in micrograms per liter in unfiltered water except as noted. mrem/yr, millirem per year; No., number; pCi/L, picocuries per liter; <, less than; --, not applicable]

Constituent	Drinking-water standard	No. of samples exceeding standard	Sand and gravel (15 samples)			Bedrock (16 samples)		
			Minimum	Median	Maximum	Minimum	Median	Maximum
Aluminum	[3]50–200	2	<3	<4	4	<3	4	948
Antimony	[1,2]6	0	<.2	<.2	.3	<.2	<.2	.4
Arsenic	[1,2]10	1	<.28	.58	14.1	<.09	.60	7.7
Barium	[1,2]2,000	0	22.6	127	266	22.7	130	1,240
Beryllium	[1,2]4	0	<.02	<.02	<.02	<.02	<.02	.05
Boron, filtered	--	--	6.6	31	473	6.3	78	439
Cadmium	[1,2]5	0	<.02	<.05	.09	<.02	<.05	.10
Chromium	[1,2]100	0	<.21	<.30	.37	<.21	<.21	14.3
Cobalt	--	--	<.02	<.02	.06	<.02	.02	1.0
Copper	[3]1,000	0	<.70	1.7	75.4	<.70	2.8	568
Iron, filtered	[2,3]300	9	<3	10	4,130	<3	138	1,950
Iron	[2,3]300	10	<5	16	4,030	23	228	8,030
Lead	[4]15	0	<.04	.08	1.03	.04	.26	2.25
Lithium	--	--	1.2	3.7	52.4	2.7	16.2	143
Manganese, filtered	[2]300 [3]50	1 12	<.2	11.1	520	.2	27.7	225
Manganese	[2]300 [3]50	1 12	<.2	10.8	531	.6	30.2	218
Molybdenum	--	--	<.1	.4	18.2	<.1	.5	7.8
Nickel	--	--	<.12	<.19	1.9	<.12	.25	10.1
Selenium	[1,2]50	0	<.05	.07	.47	<.05	<.05	.88
Silver	[2,3]100	0	<.01	<.01	<.01	<.01	<.01	.02
Strontium	--	--	55.0	158	1,680	24.7	286	19,900
Thallium	[1,2]2	0	<.06	<.06	<.30	<.06	<.06	.11
Zinc	[2,3]5,000	0	<2.4	<3.0	29.2	<2.4	5.0	215
Gross alpha radioactivity, pCi/L	[1,2]15	0	<.57	<1.1	1.9	<.5	.9	3.8
Gross beta radioactivity, pCi/L	[1,2]4 mrem/yr	--	<.63	1.6	9.8	<.65	2.0	15.0
Radon-222, pCi/L	[5]300 [6]4,000	16 0	113	510	1,880	56	290	1,310
Uranium	[1,2]30	0	<.014	.077	1.04	<.014	.066	3.31

[1]U.S. Environmental Protection Agency maximum contaminant level.

[2]New York State Department of Health maximum contaminant level.

[3]U.S. Environmental Protection Agency secondary drinking water standard.

[4]U.S. Environmental Protection Agency treatment technique.

[5]U.S. Environmental Protection Agency proposed maximum contaminant level.

[6]U.S. Environmental Protection Agency proposed alternative maximum contaminant level.

filtration analysis. The USEPA and NYSDOH MCLs for total coliform bacteria are exceeded when 5 percent of finished water samples collected in 1 month test positive for total coliform (if 40 or more samples are collected per month) or when two samples are positive for total coliform (if fewer than 40 samples are collected per month). Fecal coliform and *E. coli* were not detected in any sample. Heterotrophic plate counts ranged from less than 1 to 212 colony-forming units per milliliter (CFU/mL); the USEPA MCL (500 CFU/mL) was not exceeded.

Wells Sampled in 2006 and 2011

Six of the wells sampled in 2011 (AG 265, E1903, E1904, GS 216, OL 19, and WO 351) were sampled previously in 2006 as part of the program. Of the 147 physiochemical properties and constituents that samples were analyzed for in 2011, 141 had also been included in the analysis in 2006 (tables 1–10 through 1–13). The difference between results from 2006 and 2011 for a single well were typically smaller than those between the results from different wells. In general, there were no detectable trends in constituent concentrations between 2006 and 2011.

Summary

In 2002, the U.S. Geological Survey began an assessment of groundwater quality in bedrock and sand and gravel aquifers throughout New York State in cooperation with the New York State Department of Environmental Conservation (NYS-DEC). As a part of this assessment, portions of the Lake Erie and Niagara River Basin, the western Lake Ontario Basin, and the Allegheny River Basin in western New York were studied in 2006 and again in 2011. The 2011 study included analysis of 31 water samples collected from 16 production wells and 15 private residential wells from July through November 2011. Water samples were analyzed for 147 physiochemical properties and constituents that included major ions, nutrients, trace elements, radionuclides, pesticides, VOCs, and indicator bacteria. Six wells (AG 265, E1903, E1904, GS 216, OL 19, and WO 351) were tested in both studies, and a comparison was made of the results. The concentrations of most of the constituents changed little between 2006 and 2011.

The results indicate that groundwater generally is of acceptable quality, although at 30 of the 31 wells sampled, at least one of the following constituents was detected at a concentration that exceeded current or proposed Federal or New York State drinking-water standards: pH (two samples), sodium (eight samples), sulfate (three samples), total dissolved solids (nine samples), aluminum (two samples), arsenic (one sample), iron (ten samples), manganese (twelve samples), radon-222 (sixteen samples), benzene (one sample), and total coliform bacteria (nine samples). Existing drinking-water standards for color, chloride, fluoride, nitrate, nitrite, antimony, barium, beryllium, cadmium, chromium, copper, lead, mercury, selenium, silver, thallium, zinc, gross alpha radioactivity, uranium, fecal coliform, *Escherichia coli*, and heterotrophic bacteria were not exceeded in any of the samples collected. None of the pesticides analyzed exceeded existing drinking-water standards.

References Cited

Butch, G.K., Murray, P.M., Hebert, G.J., and Weigel, J.F., 2003, Water resources data, New York, water year 2002: U.S. Geological Survey Water-Data Report NY–02–1, p. 502–520.

Childress, C.J.O., Foreman, W.T., Connor, B.F., and Maloney, T.J., 1999, New reporting procedures based on long-term method detection levels and some considerations for interpretations of water-quality data provided by the U.S. Geological Survey National Water Quality Laboratory: U.S. Geological Survey Open-File Report 99–193, 19 p.

Coates, D.R., 1966, Glaciated Appalachian Plateau—Till shadows on hills: Science, v. 152, p. 1617–1619.

Eckhardt, D.A., Reddy, J.E., and Shaw, S.B., 2009, Groundwater quality in central New York, 2007: U.S. Geological Survey Open-File Report 2009–1257, 40 p., at http://pubs.usgs.gov/of/2009/1257/.

Eckhardt, D.A., Reddy, J.E., and Tamulonis, K.L., 2007, Ground-water quality in the Genesee River Basin, New York, 2005–06: U.S. Geological Survey Open-File Report 2007–1093, 26 p., at http://pubs.usgs.gov/of/2007/1093/.

Eckhardt, D.A., Reddy, J.E., and Tamulonis, K.L., 2008, Ground-water quality in western New York, 2006: U.S. Geological Survey Open-File Report 2008–1140, 36 p., at http://pubs.usgs.gov/of/2008/1140/.

Fisher, D.W., Isachsen, Y.W., and Rickard, L.V., 1970, Geologic map of New York State: New York State Museum Map and Chart Series no. 15, Finger Lakes and Niagara sheets, scale 1:250,000.

Hem, J.D., 1985, Study and interpretation of the chemical characteristics of natural water (3d ed.): U.S. Geological Survey Water-Supply Paper 2254, 264 p.

Hetcher-Aguila, K.K., 2005, Ground-water quality in the Chemung River Basin, New York, 2003: U.S. Geological Survey Open-File Report 04–1329, 19 p., at http://ny.water.usgs.gov/pubs/of/of041329/.

Hetcher-Aguila, K.K., and Eckhardt, D.A., 2006, Ground-water quality in the upper Susquehanna River basin, New York, 2004–05: U.S. Geological Survey Open-File Report 06–1161, 20 p., at http://pubs.usgs.gov/of/2006/1161/.

Krieger, H.L., and Whittaker, E.L., 1980, Prescribed procedures for measurement of radioactivity in drinking water: U.S. Environmental Protection Agency EPA 600/4–80–032, [not paged].

New York State Department of Health, 2011, New York State Health Department public water systems regulations: Albany, N.Y., New York State Department of Health, [variously paged], accessed January 2012, at http://www.health.state.ny.us/environmental/water/drinking/part5/tables.htm.

Nystrom, E.A., 2006, Ground-water quality in the Lake Champlain basin, New York, 2004: U.S. Geological Survey Open-File Report 06–1088, 22 p., at http://pubs.usgs.gov/of/2006/1088/.

Nystrom, E.A., 2007a, Ground-water quality in the St. Lawrence River basin, New York, 2005–2006: U.S. Geological Survey Open-File Report 2007–1066, 33 p., at http://pubs.usgs.gov/of/2007/1066/.

Nystrom, E.A., 2007b, Ground-water quality in the Delaware River Basin, New York, 2001 and 2005–2006: U.S. Geological Survey Open-File Report 2007–1098, 36 p., at http://pubs.usgs.gov/of/2007/1098/.

Nystrom, E.A., 2008, Ground-water quality in the Mohawk River Basin, New York, 2006: U.S. Geological Survey Open-File Report 2008–1086, 33 p., at http://pubs.usgs.gov/of/2008/1086/.

Nystrom, E.A., 2009, Ground-water quality in the Upper Hudson River Basin, New York, 2007: U.S. Geological Survey Open-File Report 2009–1240, 37 p., at http://pubs.usgs.gov/of/2009/1240/.

Nystrom, E.A., 2010, Groundwater quality in the Lower Hudson River Basin, New York, 2008: U.S. Geological Survey Open-File Report 2010–1197, 39 p., at http://pubs.usgs.gov/of/2010/1197/.

Nystrom, E.A., 2011, Groundwater quality in the Lake Champlain Basin, New York, 2009: U.S. Geological Survey Open-File Report 2011–1180, 42 p., at http://pubs.usgs.gov/of/2011/1180/.

Nystrom, E.A., 2012, Groundwater quality in the Delaware and St. Lawrence River Basins, New York, 2010: U.S. Geological Survey Open-File Report 2011–1320, 58 p., at http://pubs.usgs.gov/of/2011/1320/.

Nystrom, E.A., and Scott, T., 2013, Groundwater quality in the Mohawk River Basin, New York, 2011: U.S. Geological Survey Open-File Report 2013-1021, 43 p., at http://pubs.usgs.gov/of/2013/1021/.

Randall, A.D., 2001, Hydrogeologic framework of stratified-drift aquifers in the glaciated Northeastern United States: U.S. Geological Survey Professional Paper 1415–B, 179 p.

Reddy, J.E., 2012, Groundwater quality in the Genesee River Basin, New York, 2010: U.S. Geological Survey Open-File Report 2012–1135, 29 p., at http://pubs.usgs.gov/of/2012/1135/.

Reddy, J.E., and Risen, A.J., 2012, Groundwater quality in the Upper Susquehanna River Basin, New York, 2009: U.S. Geological Survey Open-File Report 2012–1045, 30 p., at http://pubs.usgs.gov/of/2012/1045/.

Risen, A.J., and Reddy, J.E., 2011a, Groundwater quality in the Eastern Lake Ontario Basin, New York, 2008: U.S. Geological Survey Open-File Report 2011–1074, 32 p., at http://pubs.usgs.gov/of/2011/1074/.

Risen, A.J., and Reddy, J.E., 2011b, Groundwater quality in the Chemung River Basin, New York, 2008: U.S. Geological Survey Open-File Report 2011–1112, 25 p., at http://pubs.usgs.gov/of/2011/1112/.

U.S. Environmental Protection Agency, 1997, Guidelines for preparation of the comprehensive state water quality assessments 305(b) reports and electronic updates: U.S. Environmental Protection Agency, EPA 841–B–97–002A and EPA 841–B–97–002B, PL 95–217, 271 p.

U.S. Environmental Protection Agency, 1999, Proposed radon in drinking water rule: U.S. Environmental Protection Agency EPA 815–F–99–006, 6 p.

U.S. Environmental Protection Agency, 2002, Drinking-water advisory—Consumer acceptability advice and health effects analysis on sodium: U.S. Environmental Protection Agency EPA 822–R–02–032, 34 p.

U.S. Environmental Protection Agency, 2009, National primary drinking water standards and national secondary drinking water standards: U.S. Environmental Protection Agency EPA 816–F–09–0004, 6 p.

U.S. Geological Survey, [variously dated], National field manual for the collection of water-quality data: U.S. Geological Survey Techniques of Water-Resources Investigations, book 9, chaps. A1–A9, at http://pubs.water.usgs.gov/twri9A/.

Appendix 1. Data Tables

Table 1–1. Information on wells sampled in western New York, 2011.

[Well locations are shown in figure 1. BLS, below land surface; ft, feet; ID, U.S. Geological Survey site identification number; no., number; —, information not available]

Well no.[1]	ID	Date sampled	Well depth, in ft BLS	Casing depth, in ft BLS	Well type[2]	Bedrock type
Sand and gravel wells						
AG 265	421300078160001	8/22/2011	70	—	P	—
CT 673	422128079025101	11/7/2011	39	31	P	—
CT 674	420126078372001	11/29/2011	78	—	P	—
CT 675	420937078410001	11/29/2011	60	—	P	—
CU 863	422112079305501	10/19/2011	—	—	P	—
CU 865	421512079161602	10/27/2011	60	58	P	—
CU1959	421024079042801	11/28/2011	45	45	D	—
CU2131	420926079355501	11/8/2011	52	32	P	—
E1903	423001078400001	9/28/2011	177	141	P	—
E1904	425424078294802	8/3/2011	45	—	P	—
E1909	423550078384201	9/29/2011	169.5	152.2	P	—
GS 216	425900078120001	8/4/2011	69	56	P	—
NI1221	431459078581201	7/27/2011	72	—	D	—
WO 351	423200078250001	9/28/2011	36	36	P	—
WO 353	424550078183901	10/26/2011	132	123.5	P	—
Bedrock wells						
AG 745	420547078055001	8/22/2011	218	46	D	Shale, siltstone, and sandstone.
CT1047	422453078441001	8/31/2011	120	54	D	Shale, siltstone, and sandstone.
CT2104	422252078324901	8/31/2011	90	20	D	Shale, siltstone, and sandstone.
CT2881	420328078265001	9/27/2011	120	82	D	Shale, siltstone, and sandstone.
CU 864	422712079182301	10/19/2011	85	—	P	Shale, siltstone, and sandstone.
CU1023	422501079200401	11/30/2011	50	8.5	D	Shale, siltstone, and sandstone.
CU2530	422923079115701	10/18/2011	85	50	D	Shale, siltstone, and sandstone.
E1312	430248078335601	8/30/2011	26	—	D	Shale, dolostone, and evaporites.
E1811	424842078294401	8/3/2011	60	20.5	D	Shale, siltstone, and sandstone.
E3393	423459078502801	7/26/2011	100	65	D	Shale, siltstone, and sandstone.
GS 479	425339078112301	9/1/2011	45	18.5	D	Shale, siltstone, and sandstone.
MO1452	431701077540801	10/25/2011	48	26	D	Shale, siltstone, and sandstone.
NI1240	430926078412801	8/23/2011	83	13	D	Limestone and dolostone.
OL 19	431230078023001	8/17/2011	32	—	P	Shale, siltstone, and sandstone.
OL 40	430828078214101	8/17/2011	75	55	P	Shale, dolostone, and evaporites.
OL 52	432022078005501	8/16/2011	25	25	D	Shale, siltstone, and sandstone.

[1]Prefix denotes county: AG, Allegany; CT, Cattaraugus; CU, Chautauqua; E, Erie; GS, Genesee; MO, Monroe; NI, Niagara; OL, Orleans; WO, Wyoming; number is local well-identification number assigned by U.S. Geological Survey.

[2]Well types: D, domestic; P, production.

Table 1–2.   Compounds for which groundwater samples from western New York were analyzed but not detected, 2011.

[A water year (WY) is the 12-month period from October 1 through September 30 of the following year; the WY is designated by the calendar year in which it ends. NWIS, U.S. Geological Survey National Water Information System]

NWIS parameter code	Constituent	Laboratory reporting level	
		WY11	WY12
Trace elements in unfiltered water, in micrograms per liter			
71900	Mercury	.005	.005
Pesticides in filtered water, in micrograms per liter			
82660	2,6-Diethylaniline	.006	.006
49260	Acetochlor	.010	.010
46342	Alachlor	.008	.008
34253	*alpha*-HCH	.004	.0040
82686	Azinphos-methyl	.120	.12
82673	Benfluralin	.014	.014
82680	Carbaryl	.060	.06
82674	Carbofuran	.060	.060
38933	Chlorpyrifos	.004	.0036
82687	*cis*-Permethrin	.010	.010
82682	DCPA	.008	.0076
62170	Desulfinyl fipronil	.012	.012
62169	Desulfinylfipronil amide	.029	.029
39572	Diazinon	.006	.0060
39381	Dieldrin	.008	.008
82677	Disulfoton	.04	.040
82668	EPTC	.006	.0056
82663	Ethalfluralin	.006	.006
82672	Ethoprop	.016	.016
62166	Fipronil	.018	.018
62167	Fipronil sulfide	.012	.012
62168	Fipronil sulfone	.024	.024
04095	Fonofos	.005	.0048
39341	Lindane	.004	.0040
82666	Linuron	.060	.06
39532	Malathion	.016	.016
82630	Metribuzin	.012	.012
82671	Molinate	.004	.0040
82684	Napropamide	.008	.008
34653	*p,p'*-DDE	.002	.002
39542	Parathion	.020	.020
82667	Methyl parathion	.008	.008
82669	Pebulate	.016	.016
82683	Pendimethalin	.012	.012
82664	Phorate	.020	.020
04024	Propachlor	.006	.006
82679	Propanil	.010	.010
82685	Propargite	.02	.020

Table 1–2. Compounds for which groundwater samples from western New York were analyzed but not detected, 2011.—Continued

[A water year (WY) is the 12-month period from October 1 through September 30 of the following year; the WY is designated by the calendar year in which it ends. NWIS, U.S. Geological Survey National Water Information System]

NWIS parameter code	Constituent	Laboratory reporting level	
		WY11	WY12
82676	Propyzamide	.004	.0036
82675	Terbufos	.02	.018
82681	Thiobencarb	.016	.016
82678	Triallate	.005	.0046
82661	Trifluralin	.018	.018
Volatile organic compounds in unfiltered water, in micrograms per liter			
77652	1,1,1-Trichloro-1,2,2-trifluoroethane	.1	.1
34496	1,1-Dichloroethane	.1	.1
34501	1,1-Dichloroethene	.1	.1
34536	1,2-Dichlorobenzene	.1	.1
34541	1,2-Dichloropropane	.1	.1
34566	1,3-Dichlorobenzene	.1	.1
34571	1,4-Dichlorobenzene	.1	.1
34301	Chlorobenzene	.1	.1
77093	*cis*-1,2-Dichloroethene	.1	.1
34668	Dichlorodifluoromethane	.2	.2
34423	Dichloromethane	.2	.2
81576	Diethyl ether	.2	.2
81577	Diisopropyl ether	.2	.2
50004	*tert*-Butyl ethyl ether	.1	.1
77135	*o*-Xylene	.1	.1
77128	Styrene	.1	.1
50005	Methyl *tert*-pentyl ether	.2	.2
32102	Tetrachloromethane	.2	.2
34546	*trans*-1,2-Dichloroethene	.1	.1
34488	Trichlorofluoromethane	.2	.2
39175	Vinyl chloride	.2	.2

Table 1–3. Physiochemical properties of groundwater samples from western New York, 2011.

[Well locations are shown in figure 1. **Bold** values exceed one or more drinking-water standard. (00080), U.S. Geological Survey (USGS) National Water Information System (NWIS) parameter code; no., number; mg/L, milligrams per liter; µS/cm @ 25 C, microsiemens per centimeter at 25 C; <, less than; C, degrees Celsius]

Well no.[1]	Water color, filtered, in platinum-cobalt units (00080)	pH, field, in standard units (00400)	Specific conductance, field, in µS/cm @ 25°C (00095)	Water temperature, in °C (00010)	Dissolved oxygen unfiltered, field, in mg/L (00300)	Dissolved nitrogen gas unfiltered, in mg/L (00597)	Carbon dioxide unfiltered, in mg/L (00405)	Methane unfiltered, in mg/L (85574)	Argon unfiltered, in mg/L (82043)	Hydrogen sulfide odor field (71875)
				Sand and gravel wells						
AG 265	<1	6.7	454	10.3	3.2	22.17	45.8	<.0005	.751	Absent
CT 673	<1	7.5	1,200	10.7	.3	26.34	33.1	.020	.7530	Absent
CT 674	<1	6.8	316	10.6	3.5	22.27	30.1	<.0005	.7780	Absent
CT 675	<1	7.7	288	12.7	3.1	18.29	8.2	<.0005	.6650	Absent
CU 863	<1	**6.0**	226	16.3	8.1	19.56	60.4	.010	.8490	Present
CU 865	<1	7.6	423	8.7	4.3	19.67	5.8	<.0005	.7150	Absent
CU1959	<1	8.2	260	12.8	7.9	20.73	1.9	<.0005	.7610	Absent
CU2131	<1	7.7	783	12.1	3.0	20.94	21.5	.002	.7290	Absent
E1903	<1	7.4	841	11.3	.4	23.39	20.9	.003	.8220	Absent
E1904	<1	7.2	1,190	12.3	.6	23.96	45.6	.056	.7780	Present
E1909	<1	8.0	276	10.3	.4	21.80	2.2	.944	.7750	Present
GS 216	<1	7.3	974	12.3	3.5	22.35	30.9	.035	.7600	Present
NI1221	<1	8.0	693	13.4	.5	25.42	3.7	.004	.8700	Absent
WO 351	<1	7.8	486	12.1	3.4	18.64	9.4	<.0005	.6830	Absent
WO 353	<1	7.9	419	10.9	.3	20.82	5.2	1.99	.7320	Present
				Bedrock wells						
AG 745	<1	6.8	138	12.0	8.1	17.71	12.0	<.0005	.6750	Absent
CT1047	<1	**8.7**	341	12.6	.8	21.41	.5	2.42	.7580	Present
CT2104	<1	7.6	421	12.1	.2	15.97	10.0	26.6	.6820	Absent
CT2881	2	7.7	365	16.4	.5	20.54	7.3	.115	.7530	Present
CU 864	<1	7.6	957	12.4	.4	6.94	6.8	29.5	.3950	Absent
CU1023	<1	7.4	625	13.1	.5	22.60	28.9	<.0005	.7530	Absent
CU2530	<1	7.7	440	13.7	.4	26.52	8.2	.069	.8130	Present
E1312	<1	7.1	1,210	17.1	.4	25.06	48.7	.008	.8060	Present
E1811	<1	7.4	543	12.0	.8	24.17	25.2	.014	.8450	Absent
E3393	<1	7.9	560	19.3	.2	12.33	4.3	24.8	.5600	Present
GS 479	<1	6.9	381	18.0	.5	22.77	34.1	<.0005	.7490	Absent
MO1452	<1	7.5	663	13.9	2.8	24.50	30.6	<.0005	.7790	Absent
NI1240	<1	7.1	2,450	12.0	.5	25.09	38.5	.058	.7570	Present
OL 19	<1	7.2	725	11.0	3.2	22.60	27.0	<.0005	.7480	Absent
OL 40	<1	7.3	1,670	11.6	.2	25.79	34.1	.033	.7760	Present
OL 52	<1	7.4	1,060	13.0	.3	28.13	27.0	.005	.7950	Absent

[1]Prefix denotes county: AG, Allegany; CT, Cattaraugus; CU, Chautauqua; E, Erie; GS, Genesee; MO, Monroe; NI, Niagara; OL, Orleans; WO, Wyoming; number is local well-identification number assigned by the USGS.

Table 1–4. Concentrations of major ions in groundwater samples from western New York, 2011.

[Well locations are shown in figure 1. **Bold** values exceed one or more drinking-water standard. CaCO₃, calcium carbonate; mg/L, milligrams per liter; no., number; (00900), U.S. Geological Survey National Water Information System (NWIS) parameter code; <, less than]

Well no.[1]	Hardness, filtered, in mg/L as CaCO₃ (00900)	Calcium, filtered, in mg/L (00915)	Magnesium, filtered, in mg/L (00925)	Potassium, filtered, in mg/L (00935)	Sodium, filtered, in mg/L (00930)	Acid-neutralizing capacity, unfiltered, in mg/L as CaCO₃ (90410)	Alkalinity, filtered, fixed endpoint, laboratory, in mg/L as CaCO₃ (29801)	Bicarbonate,[2] filtered, in mg/L (29805)	Chloride, filtered, in mg/L (00940)	Fluoride, filtered, in mg/L (00950)	Silica, filtered, in mg/L (00955)	Sulfate, filtered, in mg/L (00945)	Dissolved solids, dried at 180° Celsius, filtered, in mg/L (70300)
Sand and gravel wells													
AG 265	117	34.0	7.75	1.84	37.3	90	84	102	72.0	.07	6.56	11.9	242
CT 673	358	113	18.5	10.2	**95.9**	291	295	360	180	<.04	12.7	56.6	**671**
CT 674	108	28.8	8.83	1.02	15.3	55	55	67	55.4	.09	13.2	7.07	163
CT 675	131	44.1	4.98	1.08	9.04	116	114	139	14.9	.06	6.80	9.58	149
CU 863	68.9	20.0	4.58	1.58	14.0	37	37	45	27.0	.04	10.3	20.7	157
CU 865	162	54.2	6.40	1.68	23.3	133	139	170	41.1	.05	5.92	10.6	230
CU1959	131	40.5	7.16	.69	2.15	102	102	124	7.80	<.04	8.29	15.4	141
CU2131	281	89.5	14.0	2.41	48.5	253	245	299	93.2	.06	8.08	12.8	434
E1903	408	116	29.0	1.43	18.3	242	238	290	46.9	<.04	12.8	127	**520**
E1904	452	142	24.0	3.60	**63.0**	292	265	323	169	.07	9.39	79.0	**714**
E1909	125	35.4	8.90	.64	6.72	118	123	150	4.85	.08	14.1	172	170
GS 216	346	93.5	27.2	3.11	**60.5**	298	270	329	128	.10	8.88	241	**536**
NI1221	171	19.1	30.0	3.98	**84.5**	209	210	256	26.9	.46	12.4	114	421
WO 351	199	61.5	11.0	1.47	20.3	170	170	207	34.5	.08	7.59	16.5	267
WO 353	209	55.6	17.0	.77	9.79	176	184	224	16.0	.10	15.6	23.4	251
Bedrock wells													
AG 745	53.9	13.6	4.86	.93	3.64	42	39	48	9.58	.04	6.06	10.7	68
CT1047	7.75	2.26	.51	.77	**71.8**	121	123	150	24.0	.36	7.79	111	206
CT2104	132	38.9	8.54	1.78	36.8	194	194	237	16.6	.19	13.2	<.09	239
CT2881	145	39.7	11.2	1.86	18.9	168	172	210	6.40	.16	13.9	11.7	203
CU 864	112	32.6	7.39	3.69	**144**	208	209	255	177	.38	10.4	<.09	**502**
CU1023	288	85.3	18.1	1.81	24.2	262	262	320	30.2	.21	19.4	30.0	369
CU2530	215	68.4	10.8	.70	5.95	164	163	199	9.98	.10	13.5	53.2	251
E1312	622	189	36.7	1.43	16.7	323	318	388	32.3	.21	12.6	**307**	**874**
E1811	290	78.4	22.9	1.21	6.11	271	250	305	1.64	.10	13.4	30.6	308
E3393	64.6	17.3	5.20	2.24	**99.2**	229	230	281	42.6	.43	9.88	1.77	312
GS 479	173	55.6	8.40	.91	7.89	156	156	190	14.8	.12	7.58	12.9	213
MO1452	371	98.1	30.6	1.80	9.29	300	316	386	5.21	.14	17.7	52.7	392
NI1240	1,400	485	44.5	5.66	34.4	245	228	278	60.4	1.17	11.6	**1,240**	**2,240**
OL 19	333	92.8	24.5	2.04	17.7	247	248	303	37.2	.12	12.1	60.1	434
OL 40	717	179	65.6	2.02	**71.8**	234	235	287	173	1.16	16.9	**416**	**1,120**
OL 52	404	75.0	52.6	13.5	**61.5**	297	296	361	80.3	.18	15.6	140	**636**

[1]Prefix denotes county: AG, Allegany; CT, Cattaraugus; CU, Chautauqua; E, Erie; GS, Genesee; MO, Monroe; NI, Niagara; OL, Orleans; WO, Wyoming; number is local well-identification number assigned by the USGS.

[2]Calculated from alkalinity.

Table 1–5. Concentrations of nutrients and total organic carbon in groundwater samples from western New York study, 2011.

[Well locations are shown in figure 1. mg/L, milligrams per liter; N, nitrogen; no., number; (00623), U.S. Geological Survey (USGS) National Water Information System (NWIS) parameter code; P, phosphorus; <, less than]

Well no.[1]	Ammonia plus organic nitrogen, filtered, in mg/L as N (00623)	Ammonia, filtered, in mg/L as N (00608)	Nitrate plus nitrite, filtered, in mg/L as N (00631)	Nitrite, filtered, in mg/L as N (00613)	Orthophosphate, filtered, in mg/L as P (00671)	Total organic carbon, unfiltered, in mg/L (00680)
Sand and gravel wells						
AG 265	<.05	<.010	1.96	<.001	.025	<.3
CT 673	.28	.158	<.04	.001	<.004	1.6
CT 674	.10	<.010	.23	<.001	.035	<.5
CT 675	<.07	<.010	.71	<.001	.009	<.5
CU 863	<.07	<.010	1.32	<.001	.007	<.5
CU 865	.07	<.010	1.57	<.001	<.004	<.5
CU1959	<.07	<.010	1.44	<.001	.014	<.5
CU2131	<.07	.011	1.30	<.001	<.004	<.5
E1903	.11	.050	<.02	<.001	.010	<.3
E1904	.23	.164	.03	<.001	<.004	1.3
E1909	.12	.085	<.02	<.001	.029	<.3
GS 216	.07	.011	.62	<.001	<.004	<.3
NI1221	.26	.251	<.02	<.001	.011	.7
WO 351	.08	<.010	1.3	<.001	.009	<.3
WO 353	.22	.148	<.04	<.001	.018	<.5
Bedrock wells						
AG 745	<.05	<.010	.24	<.001	.014	<.3
CT1047	.25	.167	<.02	<.001	.031	.3
CT2104	.17	.154	<.02	<.001	.014	<.3
CT2881	.16	.103	<.02	<.001	.008	<.3
CU 864	1.2	1.01	<.04	<.001	.005	<.5
CU1023	.10	.049	.04	.005	.005	1.0
CU2530	.09	.039	<.04	<.001	<.004	<.5
E1312	.08	.017	<.02	<.001	.005	1.5
E1811	.17	.109	<.02	<.001	.004	1.1
E3393	.65	.658	<.02	<.001	.012	.3
GS 479	.15	.020	.67	.010	.004	1.9
MO1452	.12	<.010	2.74	<.001	.005	1.1
NI1240	.31	.272	.06	<.001	.006	1.0
OL 19	.07	<.010	1.76	<.001	.005	1.1
OL 40	.07	.052	.03	.001	.007	.8
OL 52	.25	.162	.09	.001	.013	1.5

[1]Prefix denotes county: AG, Allegany; CT, Cattaraugus; CU, Chautauqua; E, Erie; GS, Genesee; MO, Monroe; NI, Niagara; OL, Orleans; WO, Wyoming; number is local well-identification number assigned by the USGS.

Table 1–6. Concentrations of trace elements and radionuclides in groundwater samples from western New York, 2011.

[Well locations are shown in figure 1. **Bold** values exceed one or more drinking-water standard. µg/L, micrograms per liter; (01105), U.S. Geological Survey (USGS) National Water Information System (NWIS) parameter code; <, less than]

Well no.[1]	Aluminum, unfiltered, in µg/L (01105)	Antimony, unfiltered, in µg/L (01097)	Arsenic, unfiltered, in µg/L (01002)	Barium, unfiltered, in µg/L (01007)	Beryllium, unfiltered, in µg/L (01012)	Boron, filtered, in µg/L (01020)	Cadmium, unfiltered, in µg/L (01027)	Chromium, unfiltered, in µg/L (01034)	Cobalt, unfiltered, in µg/L (01037)	Copper, unfiltered, in µg/L (01042)	Iron, filtered, in µg/L (01046)	Iron, unfiltered, in µg/L (01045)	Lead, unfiltered, in µg/L (01051)	Lithium, unfiltered, in µg/L (01132)	Manganese, filtered, in µg/L (01056)
Sand and gravel wells															
AG 265	<3	.2	2.2	127	<.02	29	<.05	<.21	<.02	2.1	87	94	.20	1.4	**51.3**
CT 673	<4	<.2	1.4	158	<.02	87	<.02	<.30	.02	<.70	**4,130**	**4,030**	<.04	6.7	**520**
CT 674	<4	<.2	.58	22.6	<.02	31	<.02	<.30	<.02	2.7	5	16	.08	3.2	.5
CT 675	<4	<.2	.64	92.1	<.02	15	<.02	<.30	<.02	1.9	<3	11	.15	1.2	<.2
CU 863	4	<.2	<.28	244	<.02	26	.06	<.30	<.02	75.4	7	43	1.03	2.5	5.2
CU 865	<4	<.2	.30	175	<.02	19	<.02	<.30	<.02	<.70	**8**	11	.22	1.8	<.2
CU1959	<4	<.2	.89	47.3	<.02	6.6	<.02	.33	<.02	1.8	<3	6	.22	2.5	<.2
CU2131	<4	<.2	.48	108	<.02	31	.09	<.30	.04	<.70	11	7	.18	2.9	**103**
E1903	4	.3	.65	43.0	<.02	50	<.05	.29	<.02	<.70	**1,700**	**1,680**	<.18	9.0	**132**
E1904	<3	<.2	.43	211	<.02	69	<.05	<.21	.06	<.70	**640**	**652**	<.04	34.1	**84.5**
E1909	<3	<.2	.24	225	<.02	33	<.05	<.21	<.02	<.70	10	16	.05	6.1	11.1
GS 216	<3	<.2	.26	170	<.02	41	<.05	<.21	.02	1.7	6	<5	.06	8.2	.6
NI1221	<3	<.2	**14.1**	23.7	<.02	473	<.05	<.21	<.02	3.0	27	32	<.04	52.4	25.9
WO 351	<3	.2	2.9	99.1	<.02	28	<.05	.37	<.02	1.8	<3	7	.28	3.7	<.2
WO 353	<4	<.2	<.28	266	<.02	63	<.02	<.30	<.02	<.70	**433**	**427**	<.04	7.2	14.7
Bedrock wells															
AG 745	20	<.2	.26	40.1	<.02	6.3	<.05	<.21	.02	**568**	3	24	.48	2.7	.2
CT1047	43	<.2	<.09	31.4	<.02	166	<.05	<.21	<.02	<.70	13	30	.04	24.5	4.8
CT2104	4	.3	1.0	**1,170**	<.02	114	<.05	<.21	<.02	10.2	**130**	**144**	.20	22.6	**124**
CT2881	3	<.2	.48	141	<.02	106	<.05	.23	<.02	<.70	**381**	**597**	.25	17.0	**93.9**
CU 864	51	.4	<.28	**1,240**	<.02	348	<.02	<.30	.06	.85	**825**	**3,870**	**2.25**	**143**	**54.3**
CU1023	<4	<.2	.79	237	<.02	79	<.02	<.30	<.02	2.4	4	231	.16	26.7	**62.6**
CU2530	9	<.2	**36**	343	<.02	9.8	<.02	<.30	<.02	5	**507**	**576**	.14	6.5	**225**
E1312	4	<.2	1.6	22.9	<.02	78	<.05	<.21	.05	<.70	**1,950**	**1,670**	.08	11.0	26.4
E1811	**948**	<.2	**55**	414	.05	29	<.05	**14.3**	.97	38.9	**484**	**8,030**	2.1	21.8	**104**
E3393	39	<.2	<.09	667	<.02	439	<.05	<.21	<.02	1.6	220	**568**	.13	71.7	15
GS 479	5	<.2	.24	157	<.02	78	<.05	<.21	.04	3.8	<3	30	.27	10.0	2.6
MO1452	<4	<.2	.84	66.5	<.02	42	<.02	<.30	.03	3.2	14	29	.75	15.5	1.2
NI1240	<3	<.2	.80	22.7	<.02	209	<.05	<.21	.02	<.70	25	23	.04	10.8	17.4
OL 19	3	<.2	.69	118	<.02	29	<.05	<.21	.03	3.7	71	288	.96	9.40	10.1
OL 40	<3	<.2	.65	36.4	<.02	34	.10	<.21	1.0	2.2	194	224	1.22	10.4	29.0
OL 52	9	<.2	7.7	41	<.02	257	<.05	<.21	.06	3.7	146	173	.45	56.7	**76.7**

Table 1–6. Concentrations of trace elements and radionuclides in groundwater samples from western New York, 2011.

[Well locations are shown in figure 1. Bold values exceed one or more drinking-water standard. µg/L, micrograms per liter; no., number; pCi/L, picocuries per liter; (01105), U.S. Geological Survey (USGS) National Water Information System (NWIS) parameter code; <, less than]

Well no.[1]	Manganese, unfiltered, in µg/L (01055)	Molybdenum, unfiltered, in µg/L (01062)	Nickel, unfiltered, in µg/L (01067)	Selenium, unfiltered, in µg/L (01147)	Silver, unfiltered, in µg/L (01077)	Strontium, unfiltered, in µg/L (01082)	Thallium, unfiltered, in µg/L (01059)	Zinc, unfiltered, in µg/L (01092)	Gross alpha radioactivity, in pCi/L (01519)	Gross beta radioactivity, in pCi/L (85817)	Radon-222, unfiltered, in pCi/L (82303)	Uranium, unfiltered, in µg/L (28011)
Sand and gravel wells												
AG 265	**55.3**	.1	.12	.07	<.01	85.6	<.06	<2.4	<1.0	.9	**1,100**	<.014
CT 673	**531**	1.0	1.9	<.05	<.01	254	<.06	9.0	1.9	9.8	139	.892
CT 674	.5	<.1	<.19	.09	<.01	178	<.06	<3.0	<.64	1.7	**1,880**	<.014
CT 675	<.2	<.1	<.19	.06	<.01	67.9	<.06	<3.0	<.71	<.63	650	.056
CU 863	8.4	.1	1.1	.25	<.01	72.9	<.06	29.2	.6	1.4	470	<.014
CU 865	.6	<.1	<.19	.10	<.01	87.7	<.06	<3.0	<.98	1.2	670	.031
CU1959	.3	.1	<.19	.07	<.01	55.0	<.06	<3.0	1.0	.6	690	.222
CU2131	**103**	.1	<.19	.17	<.01	157	<.06	28.6	<.9	1.9	730	.262
E1903	**129**	1.8	.19	<.05	<.01	245	<.30	19.3	1.4	2.0	168	.077
E1904	**98.2**	2.9	1.1	.23	<.01	718	<.06	11.8	<1.4	2.7	133	.456
E1909	10.8	.5	<.12	<.05	<.01	158	<.06	16.4	<.57	1.4	198	<.014
GS 216	.8	1.7	.32	.47	<.01	358	<.06	4.6	<1.1	3.1	**510**	.700
NI1221	29.6	18.2	<.12	.06	<.01	1,680	<.06	<2.4	1.5	2.6	245	1.04
WO 351	.3	.4	<.12	.09	<.01	119	<.06	<2.4	<1.2	1.6	710	.177
WO 353	14.9	.5	<.19	<.05	<.01	540	<.06	<3.0	<.8	.7	113	<.014
Bedrock wells												
AG 745	.6	<.1	.23	<.05	<.01	50.3	<.06	7.3	<.5	<.65	**440**	.089
CT1047	5.2	<.1	.23	.56	<.01	24.7	<.06	<2.4	<.8	1.0	213	<.014
CT2104	**135**	.1	<.12	<.05	<.01	246	<.06	<2.4	2.7	2.4	**1,070**	<.014
CT2881	**92.8**	.4	<.12	<.05	<.01	318	<.06	<2.4	1.1	2.1	111	<.014
CU 864	**66.4**	2.1	.28	<.05	<.01	705	<.06	21.8	2.4	4.3	205	<.014
CU1023	**75.9**	.2	.27	.88	<.01	227	<.06	<3.0	<1.1	1.8	300	<.014
CU2530	**218**	.7	<.19	.11	<.01	103	<.06	10.3	.9	1.2	129	.033
E1312	26	.5	.29	.17	.02	19,900	<.06	28.2	<1.3	1.7	**320**	.084
E1811	**154**	2.5	10.1	.05	<.01	315	<.06	7.9	3.8	3.5	132	.048
E3393	16.1	.8	<.12	<.05	<.01	281	<.06	<2.4	1.5	2.3	280	<.014
GS 479	10.7	.1	.33	.05	<.01	232	<.06	<2.4	1.3	<1.4	**780**	.172
MO1452	1.5	1.3	.22	.13	<.01	291	<.06	5.2	<.86	1.6	**1,000**	1.58
NI1240	20.4	.1	.46	.88	<.01	3,650	<.06	4.7	<4.3	4.8	56	.189
OL 19	12.2	.5	.56	.11	<.01	189	<.06	6.9	<1.1	1.8	**600**	1.29
OL 40	34.5	1.3	2.2	<.05	.02	1,650	.11	215	1.8	2.2	270	.655
OL 52	**84.5**	7.8	.16	<.05	<.01	2,420	<.06	3.3	<1.5	15.0	**1,310**	3.31

[1]Prefix denotes county: AG, Allegany; CT, Cattaraugus; CU, Chautauqua; E, Erie; GS, Genesee; MO, Monroe; NI, Niagara; OL, Orleans; WO, Wyoming; number is local well-identification number assigned by the USGS.

Table 1–7.   Concentrations of pesticides detected in groundwater samples from western New York study, 2011.

[Well locations are shown in figure 1. **Bold** values indicate detected concentration. CIAT, deethylatrazine; e, estimated value (constituent was detected in the sample but with low or inconsistent recovery); M, presence verified but not quantified; µg/L, micrograms per liter; (04040), U.S. Geological Survey (USGS) National Water Information System (NWIS) parameter code; <, less than]

Well no.[1]	CIAT, filtered, in µg/L (04040)	Atrazine, filtered, in µg/L (39632)	Butylate, filtered, in µg/L (04028)	Cyanazine, filtered, in µg/L (04041)	Meto-lachlor, filtered, in µg/L (39415)	Prometon, filtered, in µg/L (04037)	Simazine, filtered, in µg/L (04035)	Tebuthiuron filtered, in µg/L (82670)	Terbacil filtered, in µg/L (82665)
					Sand and gravel wells				
AG 265	**M**	<.008	<.004	<.022	<.020	<.012	<.006	<.03	<.024
CT 673	<.006	<.008	<.004	<.022	<.020	<.012	<.006	<.03	<.024
CT 674	<.006	<.008	<.004	<.022	<.020	<.012	<.006	<.03	<.024
CT 675	**e.007**	**e.003**	<.004	<.022	<.020	**e.001**	<.006	<.03	<.024
CU 863	<.006	<.008	<.004	<.022	<.020	<.012	**M**	<.03	<.024
CU 865	**e.003**	**.007**	<.004	<.022	<.020	<.012	**.001**	<.03	<.024
CU1959	**e.015**	**e.004**	<.004	<.022	<.020	<.012	<.006	<.03	<.024
CU2131	**e.001**	**e.002**	<.004	<.022	<.020	**e.001**	<.006	<.03	<.024
E1903	<.006	<.008	<.004	<.022	<.020	<.012	<.006	<.03	<.024
E1904	<.006	<.008	<.004	<.022	<.020	<.012	<.006	<.03	<.024
E1909	<.006	<.008	<.004	<.022	<.020	<.012	<.006	<.03	<.024
GS 216	**e.005**	<.008	<.004	<.022	<.020	<.012	<.006	**.01**	<.024
NI1221	<.006	<.008	<.004	<.022	<.020	<.012	<.006	<.03	<.024
WO 351	**e.004**	<.008	<.004	<.022	<.020	<.012	<.006	<.03	<.024
WO 353	<.006	<.008	<.004	<.022	<.020	<.012	<.006	<.03	<.024
					Bedrock wells				
AG 745	**M**	<.008	<.004	<.022	<.020	<.012	<.006	<.03	<.024
CT1047	<.006	<.008	<.004	<.022	<.020	<.012	<.006	<.03	<.024
CT2104	<.006	<.008	<.004	<.022	<.020	<.012	<.006	<.03	<.024
CT2881	<.006	<.008	<.004	<.022	<.020	<.012	<.006	<.03	<.024
CU 864	<.006	<.008	<.004	<.022	<.020	<.012	<.006	<.03	<.024
CU1023	<.006	<.008	<.004	<.022	<.020	<.012	<.006	<.03	<.024
CU2530	<.006	<.008	<.004	<.022	<.020	<.012	<.006	<.03	<.024
E1312	<.006	<.008	<.004	<.022	<.020	<.012	<.006	<.03	<.024
E1811	<.006	<.008	<.004	<.022	<.020	<.012	<.006	<.03	<.024
E3393	<.006	<.008	<.004	<.022	<.020	<.012	<.006	<.03	<.024
GS 479	<.006	<.008	<.004	<.022	<.020	<.012	<.006	<.03	<.024
MO1452	**e.003**	<.008	<.004	<.022	<.020	<.012	<.006	<.03	<.024
NI1240	<.006	<.008	<.004	<.022	<.020	<.012	<.006	<.03	<.024
OL 19	**e.015**	**.032**	**.003**	**.012**	**.004**	**.004**	<.006	<.03	**e.006**
OL 40	<.006	<.008	<.004	<.022	<.020	<.012	<.006	<.03	<.024
OL 52	<.006	<.008	<.004	<.022	<.020	**.001**	<.006	<.03	<.024

[1]Prefix denotes county: AG, Allegany; CT, Cattaraugus; CU, Chautauqua; E, Erie; GS, Genesee; MO, Monroe; NI, Niagara; OL, Orleans; WO, Wyoming; number is local well-identification number assigned by the USGS.

Table 1-8.   Concentrations of volatile organic compounds in groundwater samples from western New York study, 2011.

[Well locations are shown in figure 1. **Bold** values exceed one or more drinking-water standard. µg/L, micrograms per liter; no., number; (34506), U.S. Geological Survey (USGS) National Water Information System parameter code; <, less than]

Well no.[1]	1,1,1-Trichloroethane, unfiltered, in µg/L (34506)	1,2-Dichloroethane, unfiltered, in µg/L (32103)	Benzene unfiltered, in µg/L (34030)	Bromodichloromethane, unfiltered, in µg/L (32101)	Tribromomethane, unfiltered, in µg/L (32104)	Trichloromethane, unfiltered, in µg/L (32106)	Dibromochloromethane, unfiltered, in µg/L (32105)	Ethylbenzene unfiltered, in µg/L (34371)	m- + p-Xylene, unfiltered, in µg/L (85795)	Methyl tert-butyl ether, unfiltered, in µg/L (78032)	Tetrachloroethene, unfiltered, in µg/L (34475)	Toluene, unfiltered, in µg/L (34010)	Trichloroethene, unfiltered, in µg/L (39180)
Sand and gravel wells													
AG 265	<.1	<.2	<.1	<.1	<.2	<.1	<.2	<.1	<.2	<.2	<.1	<.1	<.1
CT 673	<.1	<.2	<.1	<.1	<.2	<.1	<.2	<.1	<.2	<.2	<.1	<.1	<.1
CT 674	<.1	<.2	<.1	<.1	<.2	<.1	<.2	<.1	<.2	<.2	<.1	<.1	<.1
CT 675	<.1	<.2	<.1	<.1	<.2	<.1	<.2	<.1	<.2	<.2	<.1	<.1	<.1
CU 863	<.1	<.2	<.1	2.7	2.0	1.7	4.2	<.1	<.2	<.2	<.1	<.1	<.1
CU 865	<.1	<.2	<.1	<.1	<.2	<.1	<.2	<.1	<.2	<.2	<.1	<.1	<.1
CU1959	<.1	<.2	<.1	<.1	<.2	<.1	<.2	<.1	<.2	<.2	<.1	<.1	<.1
CU2131	.1	<.2	.1	<.1	<.2	<.1	<.2	<.1	<.2	<.2	<.1	<.1	<.1
E1903	<.1	<.2	<.1	<.1	<.2	<.1	<.2	<.1	<.2	<.2	<.1	<.1	<.1
E1904	<.1	<.2	<.1	<.1	<.2	<.1	<.2	<.1	<.2	.9	<.1	<.1	<.1
E1909	<.1	<.2	<.1	<.1	<.2	<.1	<.2	<.1	<.2	<.2	<.1	<.1	<.1
GS 216	.4	<.2	<.1	<.1	<.2	.1	<.2	<.1	<.2	<.2	.5	<.1	.2
NI1221	<.1	<.2	<.1	<.1	<.2	<.1	<.2	<.1	<.2	<.2	<.1	<.1	<.1
WO 351	<.1	<.2	<.1	<.1	<.2	<.1	<.2	<.1	<.2	<.2	<.1	<.1	<.1
WO 353	<.1	<.2	<.1	<.1	<.2	<.1	<.2	<.1	<.2	<.2	<.1	<.1	<.1
Bedrock wells													
AG 745	<.1	<.2	<.1	<.1	<.2	<.1	<.2	<.1	<.2	<.2	<.1	<.1	<.1
CT1047	<.1	<.2	<.1	<.1	<.2	.9	<.2	<.1	<.2	<.2	<.1	<.1	<.1
CT2104	<.1	<.2	<.1	<.1	<.2	<.1	<.2	<.1	<.2	<.2	<.1	<.1	<.1
CT2881	<.1	<.2	<.1	<.1	<.2	<.1	<.2	<.1	<.2	<.2	<.1	.3	<.1
CU 864	<.1	<.2	1.6	<.1	<.2	<.1	<.2	<.1	<.2	<.2	<.1	.1	<.1
CU1023	<.1	<.2	.1	<.1	<.2	<.1	<.2	<.1	<.2	<.2	<.1	<.1	<.1
CU2530	<.1	<.2	<.1	<.1	<.2	<.1	<.2	<.1	<.2	<.2	<.1	<.1	<.1
E1312	<.1	<.2	<.1	<.1	<.2	<.1	<.2	<.1	<.2	<.2	<.1	<.1	<.1
E1811	<.1	<.2	<.1	<.1	<.2	<.1	<.2	<.1	<.2	<.2	<.1	<.1	<.1
E3393	<.1	<.2	<.1	<.1	<.2	<.1	<.2	<.1	<.2	<.2	<.1	.2	<.1
GS 479	<.1	<.2	<.1	<.1	<.2	<.1	<.2	<.1	<.2	<.2	<.1	<.1	<.1
MO1452	<.1	<.2	<.1	<.1	<.2	<.1	<.2	<.1	<.2	<.2	<.1	<.1	<.1
NI1240	<.1	<.2	<.1	<.1	<.2	<.1	<.2	<.1	<.2	<.2	<.1	<.1	<.1
OL 19	<.1	<.2	<.1	<.1	<.2	<.1	<.2	<.1	<.2	<.2	<.1	.1	<.1
OL 40	<.1	<.2	<.1	<.1	<.2	<.1	<.2	<.1	<.2	<.2	<.1	<.1	<.1
OL 52	<.1	.5	**56.1**	<.1	<.2	<.1	<.2	.4	.5	.2	<.1	<.1	<.1

[1]Prefix denotes county: AG, Allegany; CT, Cattaraugus; CU, Chautauqua; E, Erie; GS, Genesee; MO, Monroe; NI, Niagara; OL, Orleans; WO, Wyoming; number is local well-identification number assigned by the USGS.

Table 1–9.   Concentrations of bacteria in unfiltered groundwater samples from western New York, 2011.

[Well locations are shown in figure 1. **Bold** values indicate detections of coliform bacteria. CFU/mL, colony-forming unit per milliliter; mL, milliliter; M, present; no., number; U, absent; (99595), U.S. Geological Survey (USGS) National Water Information System (NWIS) parameter code; —, not applicable; <, less than]

Well no.[1]	Total coliform, Colilert, presence/absence (99595)	Total coliform, membrane filtration, in colonies per 100 mL (61213)	Fecal coliform, in colonies per 100 mL (61215)	Escherichia coli, Colilert, presence/absence (99596)	Escherichia coli, in colonies per 100 mL (31691)	Heterotrophic plate count, in CFU/mL (31692)
			Sand and gravel wells			
AG 265	**M**	—	<1	U	—	13
CT 673	—	<1	<1	—	<1	4
CT 674	—	<1	<1	—	<1	4
CT 675	—	<1	<1	—	<1	2
CU 863	—	<1	<1	—	<1	2
CU 865	—	<1	<1	—	<1	3
CU1959	—	**21**	<1	—	<1	39
CU2131	—	<1	<1	—	<1	<1
E1903	—	<1	<1	—	<1	2
E1904	U	—	<1	U	—	2
E1909	—	<1	<1	—	<1	8
GS 216	U	—	<1	U	—	2
NI1221	U	—	<1	U	—	56
WO 351	—	**21**	<1	—	<1	31
WO 353	—	<1	<1	—	<1	2
			Bedrock wells			
AG 745	U	—	<1	U	—	1
CT1047	**M**	—	<1	U	—	9
CT2104	**M**	—	<1	U	—	6
CT2881	—	<1	<1	—	<1	40
CU 864	—	<1	<1	—	<1	2
CU1023	—	<1	<1	—	<1	1
CU2530	—	<1	<1	—	<1	24
E1312	**M**	—	<1	U	—	12
E1811	**M**	—	<1	U	—	212
E3393	U	—	<1	U	—	2
GS 479	U	—	<1	U	—	3
MO1452	—	**25**	<1	—	<1	41
NI1240	U	—	<1	U	—	<1
OL 19	U	—	<1	U	—	5
OL 40	U	—	<1	U	—	4
OL 52	**M**	—	<1	U	—	28

[1]Prefix denotes county: AG, Allegany; CT, Cattaraugus; CU, Chautauqua; E, Erie; GS, Genesee; MO, Monroe; NI, Niagara; OL, Orleans; WO, Wyoming; number is local well-identification number assigned by the USGS.

Table 1–10. Physiochemical properties of and concentrations of major ions, nutrients and total organic carbon, and bacteria in groundwater samples collected in western New York, 2006 and 2011.

[Well locations are shown in figure 1. **Bold** values exceed one or more drinking-water standard. CaCO₃, calcium carbonate; CFU, colony forming unit; e, estimated value—constituent was detected in the sample but with low or inconsistent recovery; M, present; mg/L, milligrams per liter; mL, milliliter; µS/cm @ 25 C, microsiemens per centimeter at 25 degrees Celsius; N, nitrogen; NWIS, U.S. Geological Survey (USGS) National Water Information System; P, phosphorus; U, absent; C, degrees Celsius; --, not applicable; <, less than]

NWIS parameter code	Constituent	AG 265[1]		E1903[1]		E1904[1]		GS 216[1]		OL 19[1]		WO 351[1]	
		2006	2011	2006	2011	2006	2011	2006	2011	2006	2011	2006	2011
00080	Color, filtered, platinum-cobalt units	5	<1	5	<1	2	<1	2	<1	2	<1	2	<1
00300	Dissolved oxygen, unfiltered, mg/L	3.0	3.2	.4	.4	.5	.6	2.1	3.5	1.0	3.2	2.6	3.4
00400	pH, unfiltered	**6.4**	6.7	7.3	7.4	7.0	7.2	7.2	7.3	7.1	7.2	7.5	7.8
00095	Specific conductance, unfiltered, µS/cm @ 25 C	495	454	830	841	1,040	1,190	1,100	974	765	725	465	486
00010	Temperature, unfiltered, degrees Celsius	12.7	10.3	11.3	11.3	13.6	12.3	12.6	12.3	12.3	11.0	12.1	12.1
00900	Hardness, filtered, mg/L as CaCO₃	140	117	420	408	480	452	400	346	380	333	200	199
00915	Calcium, filtered, mg/L	41.8	34.0	122	116	150	142	110	93.5	108	92.8	63.1	61.5
00925	Magnesium, filtered, mg/L	8.21	7.75	28.7	29.0	25.4	24.0	29.6	27.2	25.6	24.5	10.9	11.0
00935	Potassium, filtered, mg/L	1.91	1.84	1.30	1.43	3.28	3.60	3.99	3.11	2.34	2.04	1.55	1.47
00930	Sodium, filtered, mg/L	38.6	37.3	16.0	18.3	33.6	**63.0**	74.4	**60 5**	17.7	17.7	18.2	20.3
90410	Acid neutralizing capacity, unfiltered, fixed end point, lab, mg/L as CaCO₃	89	90	259	242	299	292	319	298	285	247	176	170
29801	Alkalinity, filtered, fixed end point, laboratory, mg/L as CaCO₃	89	84	259	238	299	265	318	270	284	248	176	170
29805	Bicarbonate, filtered, fixed endpoint, laboratory, mg/L	109	102	316	290	365	323	388	329	346	303	215	207
00940	Chloride, filtered, mg/L	88.0	72.0	37.9	46.9	79.9	169	140	128	41.5	37.2	29.9	34.5
00950	Fluoride, filtered, mg/L	e.08	.07	<.10	<.04	.10	.07	.14	.10	.11	.12	e.09	.08
00955	Silica, filtered, mg/L	6.31	6.56	11.8	12.8	9.67	9.39	8.96	8.88	11.8	12.1	6.75	7.59
00945	Sulfate, filtered, mg/L	12.9	11.9	136	127	135	79.0	43.6	241	63.3	60.1	17.7	16.5
70300	Dissolved solids, dried at 180 C, filtered, mg/L	272	242	**534**	**520**	**629**	**714**	**612**	**536**	462	434	258	267
00623	Ammonia plus organic-N, filtered, mg/L as N	e.06	<.05	e.10	.11	.23	.23	e.06	.07	e.09	.07	<.10	.08
00608	Ammonia, filtered, mg/L as N	<.020	<.010	.055	.050	.154	.164	e.013	.011	e.016	<.010	<.020	<.010
00631	Nitrate plus nitrite, filtered, mg/L as N	2.40	1.96	<.06	<.02	<.06	.03	.72	.62	2.33	1.76	1.38	1.3
00613	Nitrite, filtered, mg/L as N	<.002	<.001	<.002	<.001	<.002	<.001	<.002	<.001	<.002	<.001	<.002	<.001
00671	Orthophosphate, filtered, mg/L as P	.012	.025	.006	.010	e.005	<.004	e.003	<.004	.006	.005	.006	.009
00680	Total organic carbon, unfiltered, mg/L	<1.0	<.3	<1.0	<.3	1.0	1.3	<1.0	<.3	1.2	1.1	<1.0	<.3
31691	Escherichia coli, unfiltered, CFU per 100 mL	<1	--	<1	<1	<1	--	<1	--	<1	--	<1	<1
99596	Escherichia coli, Colilert, unfiltered, presence/absence	--	U	--	--	--	U	--	U	--	U	--	--
61215	Fecal coliform, unfiltered, CFU per 100 mL	<1	<1	<1	<1	<1	<1	<1	<1	<1	<1	<1	<1
31692	Heterotrophic plate count, unfiltered, CFU per mL	<2	13	17	2	19	2	2	2	3	5	10	31
61213	Total coliform, unfiltered, CFU per 100 mL	<1	--	<1	--	<1	--	<1	--	<1	--	<1	--
99595	Total coliform, Colilert, unfiltered, presence/absence	--	**M**	--	--	--	U	--	U	--	--	--	--

[1]Prefix denotes county: AG, Allegany; E, Erie; GS, Genesee; OL, Orleans; WO, Wyoming; number is local well-identification number assigned by the USGS.

Table 1–11. Concentrations of trace elements and radionuclides in groundwater samples collected in western New York, 2006 and 2011.

[Well locations are shown in figure 1. All concentrations in micrograms per liter except as noted. **Bold** values exceed one or more drinking-water standard. NWIS, U.S. Geological Survey (USGS) National Water Information System; e, estimated value—constituent was detected in the sample but with low or inconsistent recovery; pCi/L, picocuries per liter; <, less than]

NWIS parameter code	Constituent	AG 265[1] 2006	AG 265[1] 2011	E1903[1] 2006	E1903[1] 2011	E1904[1] 2006	E1904[1] 2011	GS 216[1] 2006	GS 216[1] 2011	OL 19[1] 2006	OL 19[1] 2011	WO 351[1] 2006	WO 351[1] 2011
01105	Aluminum, unfiltered	<2	<3	e2	4	<2	<3	<2	<3	<2	3	e1	<3
01097	Antimony, unfiltered	e.1	.2	<0.2	.3	<.2	<.2	<.2	<.2	<.2	<.2	<.2	.2
01002	Arsenic, unfiltered	2.2	2.2	.24	.65	.41	.43	1.3	.26	2.2	.69	3.2	2.9
01007	Barium, unfiltered	124	127	48.1	43.0	153	211	178	170	119	118	93.2	99.1
01012	Beryllium, unfiltered	<.06	<.02	<.06	<.02	<.06	<.02	<.06	<.02	<.06	<.02	<.06	<.02
01020	Boron, filtered	32	29	52	50	71	69	55	41	35	29	26	28
01027	Cadmium, unfiltered	.02	<.05	<.02	<.05	e.01	<.05	e.01	<.05	<.02	<.05	<.02	<.05
01034	Chromium, unfiltered	<.60	<.21	<.60	.29	<.60	<.21	e.40	<.21	e.38	<.21	<.60	.37
01037	Cobalt, unfiltered	.121	<.02	.245	<.02	.369	.06	.226	.02	.227	.03	.118	<.02
01042	Copper, unfiltered	31.4	2.1	1.5	<.70	e1.0	<.70	1.9	1.7	6.6	3.7	2.2	1.8
01046	Iron, filtered	28	87	**1,630**	**1,700**	**888**	**640**	<6	6	**304**	71	e3	<3
01045	Iron, unfiltered	187	94	**1,540**	**1,680**	**806**	**652**	e4	<5	316	288	27	7
01051	Lead, unfiltered	1.64	.20	e.04	<.18	<.06	<.04	.07	.06	.12	.96	.33	.28
01132	Lithium, unfiltered	1.2	1.4	8.5	9.0	28.5	34.1	10.2	8.2	7.4	9.40	2.9	3.7
01056	Manganese, filtered	**57.5**	**51.3**	**136**	**132**	**107**	**84.5**	e.5	.6	28.0	10.1	<.6	<.2
01055	Manganese, unfiltered	**67.1**	**55.3**	**133**	**129**	**107**	**98.2**	e.4	.8	27.7	12.2	<.6	.3
01062	Molybdenum, unfiltered	.1	.1	1.9	1.8	2.6	2.9	1.6	1.7	.4	.5	.4	.4
01067	Nickel, unfiltered	1.16	.12	.86	.19	2.52	1.1	.87	.32	.66	.56	.31	<.12
01147	Selenium, unfiltered	e.07	.07	<.08	<.05	.54	.23	.8	.47	.27	.11	.23	.09
01077	Silver, unfiltered	.06	<.01	<.02	<.01	<.02	<.01	<.02	<.01	<.02	<.01	<.02	<.01
01082	Strontium, unfiltered	94.1	85.6	237	245	631	718	364	358	189	189	111	119
01059	Thallium, unfiltered	<.18	<.06	<.18	<.30	<.18	<.06	<.18	<.06	<.18	<.06	<.18	<.06
01092	Zinc, unfiltered	196	<2.4	39	19.3	16	11.8	7	4.6	6	6.9	3	<2.4
82303	Radon-222, unfiltered, pCi/L	**1,200**	**1,100**	190	168	170	133	**470**	**510**	**540**	**600**	**680**	**710**
28011	Uranium, unfiltered	.017	<.014	.074	.077	.473	.456	.837	.700	.72	1.29	.17	.177

[1]Prefix denotes county: AG, Allegany; E, Erie; GS, Genesee; OL, Orleans; WO, Wyoming; number is local well-identification number assigned by the USGS.

Table 1–12.   Concentrations of pesticides in groundwater samples collected in western New York, 2006 and 2011.

[Well locations are shown in figure 1. All concentrations in micrograms per liter in filtered water. **Bold** values indicate detected concentration. e, estimated value—constituent was detected in the sample but with low or inconsistent recovery; M, presence verified but not quantified; NWIS, U.S. Geological Survey (USGS) National Water Information System; <, less than]

NWIS parameter code	Constituent	AG 265[1] 2006	AG 265[1] 2011	E1903[1] 2006	E1903[1] 2011	E1904[1] 2006	E1904[1] 2011	GS 216[1] 2006	GS 216[1] 2011	OL 19[1] 2006	OL 19[1] 2011	WO 351[1] 2006	WO 351[1] 2011
82660	2,6-Diethylaniline	<.006	<.006	<.006	<.006	<.006	<.006	<.006	<.006	<.006	<.006	<.006	<.006
04040	2-Chloro-4-isopropylamino-6-amino-s-triazine (CIAT)	<.014	M	<.014	<.006	<.014	<.006	**e.005**	**e.005**	**e.019**	**e.015**	**e.005**	**e.004**
49260	Acetochlor	<.006	<.010	<.006	<.010	<.006	<.010	<.006	<.010	<.006	<.010	<.006	<.010
46342	Alachlor	<.005	<.008	<.005	<.008	<.005	<.008	<.005	<.008	<.005	<.008	<.005	<.008
34253	alpha-HCH	<.005	<.004	<.005	<.004	<.005	<.004	<.005	<.004	<.005	<.004	<.005	<.004
39632	Atrazine	<.007	<.008	<.007	<.008	<.007	<.008	<.007	<.008	**.026**	**.032**	<.007	<.008
82686	Azinphos-methyl	<.050	<.120	<.050	<.120	<.050	<.120	<.050	<.120	<.050	<.120	<.050	<.120
82673	Benfluralin	<.006	<.014	<.006	<.014	<.006	<.014	<.006	<.014	<.006	<.014	<.006	<.014
04028	Butylate	<.004	<.004	<.004	<.004	<.004	<.004	<.004	<.004	<.004	**.003**	<.004	<.004
82680	Carbaryl	<.041	<.060	<.041	<.060	<.041	<.060	<.041	<.060	<.041	<.060	<.041	<.060
82674	Carbofuran	<.020	<.060	<.020	<.060	<.020	<.060	<.020	<.060	<.020	<.060	<.020	<.060
38933	Chlorpyrifos	<.005	<.004	<.005	<.004	<.005	<.004	<.005	<.004	<.005	<.004	<.005	<.004
82687	cis-Permethrin	<.006	<.010	<.006	<.010	<.006	<.010	<.006	<.010	<.006	<.010	<.006	<.010
04041	Cyanazine	<.018	<.022	<.018	<.022	<.018	<.022	<.018	<.022	<.018	**.012**	<.018	<.022
82682	DCPA	<.003	<.008	<.003	<.008	<.003	<.008	<.003	<.008	<.003	<.008	<.003	<.008
62170	Desulfinylfipronil	<.012	<.012	<.012	<.012	<.012	<.012	<.012	<.012	<.012	<.012	<.012	<.012
39572	Diazinon	<.005	<.006	<.005	<.006	<.005	<.006	<.005	<.006	<.005	<.006	<.005	<.006
39381	Dieldrin	<.009	<.008	<.009	<.008	<.009	<.008	<.009	<.008	<.009	<.008	<.009	<.008
82677	Disulfoton	<.02	<.04	<.02	<.04	<.02	<.04	<.02	<.04	<.02	<.04	<.02	<.04
82668	EPTC	<.004	<.006	<.004	<.006	<.004	<.006	<.004	<.006	<.004	<.006	<.004	<.006
82663	Ethalfluralin	<.009	<.006	<.009	<.006	<.009	<.006	<.009	<.006	<.009	<.006	<.009	<.006
82672	Ethoprop	<.005	<.016	<.005	<.016	<.005	<.016	<.005	<.016	<.005	<.016	<.005	<.016
62169	Desulfinylfipronil amide	<.029	<.029	<.029	<.029	<.029	<.029	<.029	<.029	<.029	<.029	<.029	<.029
62167	Fipronil sulfide	<.013	<.012	<.013	<.012	<.013	<.012	<.013	<.012	<.013	<.012	<.013	<.012
62168	Fipronil sulfone	<.024	<.024	<.024	<.024	<.024	<.024	<.024	<.024	<.024	<.024	<.024	<.024
62166	Fipronil	<.016	<.018	<.016	<.018	<.016	<.018	<.016	<.018	<.016	<.018	<.016	<.018
04095	Fonofos	<.003	<.005	<.003	<.005	<.003	<.005	<.003	<.005	<.003	<.005	<.003	<.005
39341	Lindane	<.004	<.004	<.004	<.004	<.004	<.004	<.004	<.004	<.004	<.004	<.004	<.004
82666	Linuron	<.060	<.060	<.060	<.060	<.060	<.060	<.060	<.060	<.060	<.060	<.060	<.060
39532	Malathion	<.016	<.016	<.016	<.016	<.016	<.016	<.016	<.016	<.016	<.016	<.016	<.016
82667	Methyl parathion	<.015	<.008	<.015	<.008	<.015	<.008	<.015	<.008	<.015	<.008	<.015	<.008
39415	Metolachlor	<.010	<.020	<.010	<.020	<.010	<.020	<.010	<.020	**e.002**	**.004**	<.010	<.020
82630	Metribuzin	<.006	<.012	<.006	<.012	<.006	<.012	<.006	<.012	<.006	<.012	<.006	<.012
82671	Molinate	<.003	<.004	<.003	<.004	<.003	<.004	<.003	<.004	<.003	<.004	<.003	<.004

Table 1–12. Concentrations of pesticides in groundwater samples collected in western New York, 2006 and 2011.—Continued

[Well locations are shown in figure 1. All concentrations in micrograms per liter in filtered water. **Bold** values indicate detected concentration. e, estimated value—constituent was detected in the sample but with low or inconsistent recovery; M, presence verified but not quantified; NWIS, U.S. Geological Survey (USGS) National Water Information System; <, less than]

NWIS parameter code	Constituent	AG 265[1] 2006	AG 265[1] 2011	E1903[1] 2006	E1903[1] 2011	E1904[1] 2006	E1904[1] 2011	GS 216[1] 2006	GS 216[1] 2011	OL 19[1] 2006	OL 19[1] 2011	WO 351[1] 2006	WO 351[1] 2011
82684	Napropamide	<.007	<.008	<.007	<.008	<.007	<.008	<.007	<.008	<.007	<.008	<.007	<.008
34653	*p,p'*-DDE	<.003	<.002	<.003	<.002	<.003	<.002	<.003	<.002	<.003	<.002	<.003	<.002
39542	Parathion	<.010	<.020	<.010	<.020	<.010	<.020	<.010	<.020	<.010	<.020	<.010	<.020
82669	Pebulate	<.004	<.016	<.004	<.016	<.004	<.016	<.004	<.016	<.004	<.016	<.004	<.016
82683	Pendimethalin	<.022	<.012	<.022	<.012	<.022	<.012	<.022	<.012	<.022	<.012	<.022	<.012
82664	Phorate	<.011	<.020	<.011	<.020	<.011	<.020	<.011	<.020	<.011	<.020	<.011	<.020
04037	Prometon	<.01	<.012	<.01	<.012	<.01	<.012	<.01	<.012	<.01	**.004**	<.01	<.012
82676	Propyzamide	<.004	<.004	<.004	<.004	<.004	<.004	<.004	<.004	<.004	<.004	<.004	<.004
04024	Propachlor	<.010	<.006	<.010	<.006	<.010	<.006	<.010	<.006	<.010	<.006	<.010	<.006
82679	Propanil	<.011	<.010	<.011	<.010	<.011	<.010	<.011	<.010	<.011	<.010	<.011	<.010
82685	Propargite	<.02	<.02	<.02	<.02	<.02	<.02	<.02	<.02	<.02	<.02	<.02	<.02
04035	Simazine	<.006	<.006	<.006	<.006	<.006	<.006	<.006	<.006	<.006	<.006	<.006	<.006
82670	Tebuthiuron	<.02	<.03	<.02	<.03	<.02	<.03	<.02	**.01**	<.02	<.03	<.02	<.03
82665	Terbacil	<.034	<.024	<.034	<.024	<.034	<.024	<.034	<.024	<.034	**e.006**	<.034	<.024
82675	Terbufos	<.02	<.02	<.02	<.02	<.02	<.02	<.02	<.02	<.02	<.02	<.02	<.02
82681	Thiobencarb	<.010	<.016	<.010	<.016	<.010	<.016	<.010	<.016	<.010	<.016	<.010	<.016
82678	Triallate	<.006	<.005	<.006	<.005	<.006	<.005	<.006	<.005	<.006	<.005	<.006	<.005
82661	Trifluralin	<.009	<.018	<.009	<.018	<.009	<.018	<.009	<.018	<.009	<.018	<.009	<.018

[1]Prefix denotes county: AG, Allegany; E, Erie; GS, Genesee; OL, Orleans; WO, Wyoming; number is local well-identification number assigned by the USGS.

Table 1–13. Concentrations of volatile organic compounds in groundwater samples collected in western New York, 2006 and 2011.

[Well locations are shown in figure 1. All concentrations in micrograms per liter in unfiltered water. **Bold** values indicate detected concentration. e, estimated value—constituent was detected in the sample but with low or inconsistent recovery; NWIS, U.S. Geological Survey (USGS) National Water Information System; <, less than]

NWIS parameter code	Constituent	AG 265[1]		E1903[1]		E1904[1]		GS 216[1]		OL 19[1]		WO 351[1]	
		2006	2011	2006	2011	2006	2011	2006	2011	2006	2011	2006	2011
34506	1,1,1-Trichloroethane	<.1	<.1	<.1	<.1	<.1	<.1	**.6**	**.4**	<.1	<.1	<.1	<.1
77652	1,1,2-Trichloro-1,2,2-trifluo-roethane (CFC–113)	<.1	<.1	<.1	<.1	<.1	<.1	<.1	<.1	<.1	<.1	<.1	<.1
34496	1,1-Dichloroethane	<.1	<.1	<.1	<.1	<.1	<.1	**.1**	<.1	<.1	<.1	<.1	<.1
34501	1,1-Dichloroethene	<.1	<.1	<.1	<.1	<.1	<.1	<.1	<.1	<.1	<.1	<.1	<.1
34536	1,2-Dichlorobenzene	<.1	<.1	<.1	<.1	<.1	<.1	<.1	<.1	<.1	<.1	<.1	<.1
32103	1,2-Dichloroethane	<.2	<.2	<.2	<.2	<.2	<.2	<.2	<.2	<.2	<.2	<.2	<.2
34541	1,2-Dichloropropane	<.1	<.1	<.1	<.1	<.1	<.1	<.1	<.1	<.1	<.1	<.1	<.1
34566	1,3-Dichlorobenzene	<.1	<.1	<.1	<.1	<.1	<.1	<.1	<.1	<.1	<.1	<.1	<.1
34571	1,4-Dichlorobenzene	<.1	<.1	<.1	<.1	<.1	<.1	<.1	<.1	<.1	<.1	<.1	<.1
34030	Benzene	<.1	<.1	<.1	<.1	<.1	<.1	<.1	<.1	<.1	<.1	<.1	<.1
32101	Bromodichloromethane	<.1	<.1	<.1	<.1	<.1	<.1	<.1	<.1	<.1	<.1	<.1	<.1
32104	Tribromomethane	<.2	<.2	<.2	<.2	<.2	<.2	<.2	<.2	<.2	<.2	<.2	<.2
34301	Chlorobenzene	<.1	<.1	<.1	<.1	<.1	<.1	<.1	<.1	<.1	<.1	<.1	<.1
77093	cis-1,2-Dichloroethene	<.2	<.1	<.2	<.1	<.2	<.1	<.2	<.1	<.2	<.1	<.2	<.1
32105	Dibromochloromethane	**e.1**	<.2	<.2	<.2	<.2	<.2	<.2	<.2	<.2	<.2	<.2	<.2
34668	Dichlorodifluoromethane	<.2	<.2	<.2	<.2	<.2	<.2	<.2	<.2	<.2	<.2	<.2	<.2
34423	Dichloromethane	<.2	<.2	<.2	<.2	<.2	<.2	<.2	<.2	<.2	<.2	<.2	<.2
81576	Diethyl ether	<.2	<.2	<.2	<.2	<.2	<.2	<.2	<.2	<.2	<.2	<.2	<.2
81577	Diisopropyl ether	<.2	<.2	<.2	<.2	<.2	<.2	<.2	<.2	<.2	<.2	<.2	<.2
34371	Ethylbenzene	<.1	<.1	<.1	<.1	<.1	<.1	<.1	<.1	<.1	<.1	<.1	<.1
50005	Methyl tert-pentyl ether	<.2	<.2	<.2	<.2	<.2	<.2	<.2	<.2	<.2	<.2	<.2	<.2
85795	m- + p-Xylene	<.2	<.2	<.2	<.2	<.2	<.2	<.2	<.2	<.2	<.2	<.2	<.2
77135	o-Xylene	<.1	<.1	<.1	<.1	<.1	<.1	<.1	<.1	<.1	<.1	<.1	<.1
77128	Styrene	<.1	<.1	<.1	<.1	<.1	<.1	<.1	<.1	<.1	<.1	<.1	<.1
50004	tert-Butyl ethyl ether	<.2	<.1	<.2	<.1	<.2	<.1	<.2	<.1	<.2	<.1	<.2	<.1
78032	Methyl tert-butyl ether (MTBE)	<.2	<.2	<.2	<.2	**1.3**	**.9**	<.2	<.2	<.2	<.2	<.2	<.2
34475	Tetrachloroethene	**.2**	<.1	<.1	<.1	<.1	<.1	**.4**	**.5**	<.1	<.1	<.1	<.1
32102	Tetrachloromethane	<.1	<.2	<.1	<.2	<.1	<.2	<.1	<.2	<.1	<.2	<.1	<.2
34010	Toluene	<.1	<.1	<.1	<.1	<.1	<.1	<.1	<.1	<.1	**.1**	<.1	<.1
34546	trans-1,2-Dichloroethene	<.1	<.1	<.1	<.1	<.1	<.1	<.1	<.1	<.1	<.1	<.1	<.1
39180	Trichloroethene	<.1	<.1	<.1	<.1	<.1	<.1	**.3**	**.2**	<.1	<.1	<.1	<.1
34488	Trichlorofluoromethane (CFC–11)	<.1	<.2	<.1	<.2	<.1	<.2	<.1	<.2	<.1	<.2	<.1	<.2
32106	Trichloromethane	<.1	<.1	<.1	<.1	<.1	<.1	**.3**	**.1**	<.1	<.1	<.1	<.1
39175	Vinyl chloride	<.2	<.2	<.2	<.2	<.2	<.2	<.2	<.2	<.2	<.2	<.2	<.2

[1]Prefix denotes county: AG, Allegany; E, Erie; GS, Genesee; OL, Orleans; WO, Wyoming; number is local well-identification number assigned by the USGS.